FOREWORD BY
INTERNATIONAL LEADERSHIP EXPERT
DENNIS D. SEMPEBWA, PH. D.

The Wilderness

A PLACE OF PREPARATION

THE MAKING OF SONS

The Wilderness

A Place of Preparation

The Making of Sons

Deborah G. Hunter

Hunter Heart Publishing
Colorado Springs, Colorado

To order products, or for any other correspondence:

Hunter Heart Publishing
4164 Austin Bluffs Parkway, Suite 214
Colorado Springs, Colorado 80918
www.hunterheartpublishing.com
Tel. (253) 906-2160 – Fax: (719) 528-6359
E-mail: publisher@hunterheartpublishing.com
Or reach us on the internet: www.hunterheartpublishing.com

"Offering God's Heart to a Dying World"

This book and all other Hunter Heart Publishing™ books are available at Christian bookstores and distributors worldwide.

Chief Editor: Gord Dormer
Book cover design: Phil Coles Independent Design
Layout & logos: Exousia Marketing Group www.exousiamg.com

ISBN: 978-1-937741-73-0
Printed in the United States of America.

Dedication

I want to dedicate this book and this process solely to my Lord and Savior, Jesus Christ. I have found that though there are many voices who have poured into my life, given me advice and counsel, and who have labored in prayer and intercession for me, there is but ONE who has held me in the palm of His hand. He kept me when I wanted my life to end, He covered me when the gates of hell surrounded me, He comforted me when all had left me, He avenged me when my accusers were many, and He lifted me when it was time to put His words in my mouth. He is my Lord, my Rock, my Savior, my Redeemer, my Healer, my Provider, my Banner, my Shield, my Lion, my Lamb…..HE IS GOD!

In Loving Memory of Daryl Johnson

(March 1, 1974-December 9, 2013)

Acknowledgments

Throughout my journey, over the last fifteen years of serving the Lord, God has strategically placed people in my life to encourage, equip, and exhort…comfort, chastise, and correct… teach, toil, and train…and to prepare, pronounce, and prophesy into my life. Each of them was obedient in the seasons they were assigned to my life, and I am eternally grateful to everyone who felt it not robbery to sow into my destiny, directly or indirectly!

~Apostle Steven W. & Dr. Keira Taylor-Banks
~Pastors Daryl & Linda Magee
~Drs Will & Kristie Moreland
~Drs Casey & Wendy Treat
~Pastor Bill Lagerquist
~Kennethea Neal (In the arms of our Heavenly Father-2008)
~Dr. Dennis Sempebwa
~Pastor Pietro Evangelista
~Dr. Joe Ibojie
~Hilary Amara
~Pastora Mariet Perez
~Don Nori, Sr.
~Jana Mitten
~Angie Shields
~Ruby James
~Neechy Dumas
~Brenda Mates
~Pastors Andre & Anitress Chambers
~LaShorne Zarlengo
~Rev. Dr. E. Christopher & Lady Joy Hill

Endorsements

"As we travel throughout our lives, we learn various lessons within the varied seasons we encounter. Lifelong learners are able to capture the many lessons we encounter within these seasons. Deborah Hunter has captured not only seasons and times, but she has skillfully identified and located these destiny places we all have, or will, encounter. *The Wilderness* is well-researched with a profound accruement and insight not only into Biblical geography, but keen spiritual applications of these places within all of our lives.

For me personally, this is much more than a masterpiece, it serves as a benchmark in which I've had the honor and privilege of celebrating, cheering, and even crying with this amazing author over the years. The biblical research is documented, the spiritual application is sound, but I commend to you one of the purest hearts you will ever encounter. Her love and commitment to her spiritual maturation, her family and her Kingdom assignment is not only depicted in and through this book, but more importantly it is made visible in her daily life through her interaction with people from many diverse backgrounds and walks of life.

The Wilderness will not only inspire you on your journey, but it will bring meaningful understanding to assist in the developmental process of producing healthy and prepared sons and daughters for the Kingdom. I'm elated to fully and wholeheartedly endorse my spiritual daughter, Deborah Hunter, as a vessel who has and continues to endure the process."

Steven W. Banks
Author, Consultant, Spiritual Father
Healing the Father-Wound
Atlanta, GA

As you open the pages of this book you will journey into Deborah Hunter's field of deep, mature revelation. GET READY TO GLEAN! Prepare to find valuable precious jewels, nuggets of profound wisdom, and to walk through the refiner's fire. Go ahead and plan to host your own coming out party, as you come out on the other side of "THE WILDERNESS".

This comprehensive treatise will allow you to rest and trust through these inevitable seasons of life with a profound appreciation for the process, and an embracing of Our Saviour, as HIS WORD leads you out to victory. The phrase "life-changing" is so overused, but for me, a night with this book---produced a "suddenly" affirming affect on me. I will never be the same. Thank you Deborah, for paying the costly price that qualifies you to be a TRUE ENCOURAGER!

Now, be coached to victory through the divine strategy that only comes to those who have navigated "THE WILDERNESS" at the feet of Jesus, for in this book, He is the star. ~Jana Mitten, Worshipper

Jana Mitten
Worship leader at Solid Rock Church Cincinnati, OH
National Recording Artist, Jana Mitten & The Fire Choir

"We are born with a purpose, a unique genius, and a predestined plan for our lives. But just like the ingredients for a cake, we must go through a process in order to serve the world with our purpose and genius. Deborah, with great care and skill, shares her personal process she calls *The Wilderness*. Learn from this book, lean on this book, and leverage the wisdom in this book. Anyone that truly wants to make an impact in the world must go through the wilderness."

Dr. Will Moreland
America's #1 Leadership Life Trainer
President of Will Moreland International
Phoenix, AZ

"I stand in awe of Deborah's honesty, determination, and courage in "Speaking the Truth," and the majesty of her loving, not just of God, but of life, and of hard-won integrity, as she shares the steps of a journey in *The Wilderness* that no one wants to take. We don't always get to choose what happens in this life, but we can choose to grow in compassion and wisdom as a result. This is a lovely book, a moving account of a difficult journey, full of heart and wisdom."

Pastora Mariet Perez
Pastor of Bamberg Christian Center
Bamberg, Germany

"The Wilderness is the place where, more likely, we are able to silently listen to God's still voice; the only place where we see our-selves, others, and God in their respective ways. No wonder, talking about Israel, God said, "Therefore, behold, I will allure her, Will bring her into the wilderness, And speak comfort to her." (Hosea 2:14, NKJV) I thank God for Deborah who has been courageous enough to candidly and honestly talk about her own experience in such a place."

Pastor Pietro Evangelista
Publisher, Evangelista Media Christian Publishing House
Pescara, Italy

"I am no rebel...I am a submitted woman who has been through her wilderness."

~Deborah G. Hunter

Table of Contents

Foreword

"Dr. Dennis, I need breakthrough...it feels like God is stretching me." Deborah's tone of voice seemed different, even shaky. Over the years, we had prayed through various crises and seen the Hand of God. But something was markedly different about her plea. "Help your servant Lord," I whispered. Several weeks later, we spoke again. "Sir, I need God. It's like all hell has broken loose. My kids, my health, my marriage, my church, my business...I am being attacked from every side. Even my reputation, which I protect so passionately, is being tarnished and no matter what I do, it seems to only get worse. I am seeking God for answers, but even He seems distant. Crazy as it sounds, I do feel His presence, but I just can't seem to be able to shake this attack."

Aha...there, I knew it! The darkness, the cold, the isolation, the desolation, the endless questions...all typical of a wilderness. Deborah was in a wilderness! Since I was just coming out of one myself, I could still smell the distinctive aroma of that unique vegetation. I had to explain to my weary friend that no fervency of prayer, length of fasting, depth of scriptural insight, profoundness of wisdom, or level of anointing would change her station. This was not a season to be overcome, rebuked, prayed, or confessed away, but endured. Deborah was to take her notepad and with her bruised hands, chronicle her journey. She was to brace for the cold stretch, the endless echoing questions, and the bitter anguish of unlearning that must come from this breaking season. She was to focus on the fruit - the lush rare fruit that ONLY grows in the wilderness. This remarkable book is the glowing result of her voyage.

After decades of digesting simplistic, formulaic, hyper-faith theology that teaches us to only expect a pain-free, stress-free, problem-free, hassle-free "heritage," keen observers can now clearly see the spiritual devastation – weak, over-gratified, whiny, spoiled brats! Many of us are shipwrecked, because we thought God would do what we wanted, when we wanted, and how we wanted. What a sad delusion! The fact is patience, temperance, character, kindness, goodness,

The Wilderness

courage, and even faith ONLY come by way of adversity, setbacks, and pressure – the wilderness! Paul wrote, "Not only so, but we also glory in our sufferings, because we know that suffering produces perseverance; perseverance character; and character, hope." (Romans 5:3, 4)

When Deborah first asked me to write this foreword, I wanted to decline. I didn't think I could do it without succumbing to the limitations of my experience and intellect. I knew that she wasn't looking for an academic treatise on this vital subject. I had heard her anguished woes. This book isn't a theoretic exercise, but a very personal and precious testament of Deborah's priceless journey. Thus, allow me to invite you to open your heart as you scroll through these pages.

THE WILDERNESS is a must-read. It is an invitation to embrace the perplexing contradiction of victorious brokenness, which forms the critical birthing place of great character and true wholeness. May it cause you to find that place of settling, as you allow the Potter to make you the beautiful vessel He has in mind.

Dennis D. Sempebwa, DMin, PhD.
President & Founder: Eagle's Wings International
President & CEO: Dominion Consultancy
Dallas, TX
USA

"The Wilderness is the place of Preparation for your Promise."

~Deborah G. Hunter

Prologue

Each of us was created with a purpose; a predestined plan by our Heavenly Father to carry out His Will in this earth. The sheer awe that we were on the mind of God before we were even formed in our mother's womb....undoubtedly astounding! The Word of God in Psalm 8:4 says it so magnificently, "What is man that You are mindful of him, And the son of man that You visit him?" David, in this psalm to the Lord, tried, with his natural mind to understand how, and yes, even why, the Creator of the Universe would take the time not only to create a people, but to form purpose and individual destiny inside of each and every one of them. How many times do we brush off our existence as unimportant, or unnecessary in the sketch of God's intent for this earth? How often do we look at others and so easily see that they possess greatness within and that they are destined with purpose, but refuse to observe this in our own lives?

When Heaven invades earth and purpose intersects with destiny, the process towards your promise begins. So often, we are summoned to receive ALL that God has for us; to just believe by faith

The Wilderness

that we can have what we say and that anything we ask in His name, we can possess, but where are we being taught that there is a crucial bridge in between the proclamation and the promise? How often do we hear that God wants us to prosper, but there is not mention of the process it will take to sustain the kind of prosperity God desires in and through our lives? Over and over again, we heed the voices that tell us we can be healed, but refuse to remind us that forgiveness is critical in the manifesting of this promise? Why do we teach the blessing of God without brokenness? The favor of God without faithfulness? Success without suffering? We are forsaking the full counsel of the Lord in an effort to draw people into the kingdom of God, but we are, sad to say, causing more harm than good. The Word of the Lord is fully and inexplicably self-sufficient in its effort to woo the believer not only by grace, but also through Truth. "For the law was given through Moses, but grace and truth came through Jesus Christ." (John 1:17) Much too often, these days, we desire to hear about the grace of God, but fail to seek the truth of His Word that penetrates our hearts and reveals the true nature of who we are, so that we can be transformed. The Bible says that it is "living and powerful, and sharper than any two-edged sword, piercing even to the division of soul and spirit, and of joints and marrow, and is a discerner of the thoughts and intents of the heart." (Hebrews 4:12)

If people are to be renewed and transformed, and subsequently positioned for their purpose, they must be taught and fully understand that the process is absolutely pertinent to them receiving the full promise of God for their lives. To grow fully the believer in Christ, the disciple of the Lord... the sons of God, we must offer the entirety of God's counsel through His infallible Word. We cannot skip the course of tests, trials, and tribulation that is assured will come if we are to become entirely what God has purposed for us. We need the meat of the Word to break us, shape us, mold us, and form us. He is the potter and we are the clay. Those who avoid this transformation and see themselves as righteous set themselves up for ultimate failure and devastation. Many want to be used by God, but reject His work in their lives. We desire titles, positions, wealth, notoriety, fame, blessing, and favor, but decline to allow Him to build the character, integrity, and wisdom we really need to navigate towards our purpose. We want these "things", but don't understand that without the process, these "things" can overtake us and cause us to fall away from Him. There needs to be an adequate balance in our lives that supplies the grace, or room, for us to fail, as well as the truth that provides accountability, structure, and discipline to grow us as disciples, and subsequently.....sons of God.

My prayer is that we would seek, once again, the fullness of His Word and rely totally upon Holy Spirit to lead us, guide us, and direct us towards the promise of God for our lives and for His Church, His Kingdom, in the earth. This life is not about us, but wholly about fulfilling His purpose through us. If you find yourself in a place of great uncertainty, a place where you feel you have served God faithfully, but sense a 'falling away' of sorts, or a position of stagnancy, loneliness, or even darkness, then you may very well be in your "Wilderness". Don't fight the process. Let God form His perfect will in your life, so that He can use you for His glory.

Chapter 1

Predestined For Purpose

"The Wilderness of Egypt"
(The Place of Temptation)

"Before I formed you in the womb I knew you; Before you were born I sanctified you; I ordained you a prophet to the nations."

Jeremiah 1:5

Who am I? Why am I here? What do I have to offer this world? How can God use such a messed up person like me? These are questions that most people ask themselves at least once in their lifetime. The scope of uncertainty is exceptionally valid and comprehensible. How can one explain the vastness of this earth, let alone the expanse of the Universe, and their role on the stage of life? So many look to others' lives as being important and beneficial to the growth and expansion of this world, but cannot for the life of them see themselves

The Wilderness

as valuable. They view others as possessing the gifts, talents, and abilities to really make a difference, but only see themselves as a speck in the journey we call life. Many children are not raised to know they have purpose, or that they were created for a specific purpose in mind. Too often, generations of families pass down to their children the mindset of "existence", as opposed to purposefully living the lives God predestined for us all to live. One definition of exist means to live an unsatisfactory, joyless, or humdrum life, as opposed to an exciting or meaningful one; simply existing from day to day. How many of us find ourselves in these words? We are frustrated and angry at the hand we were dealt in this life and feel as if we are struggling to find something better; something that will bring us joy and contentment. This existence is compromisingly detrimental to the life of any human being. We were created for greatness. We were formed with purpose in mind. We were fashioned by the hand of the Creator, each uniquely designed by the master Craftsman of the universe to make our mark and leave an impact in this world for Him.

When we look at the life of Joseph, the shepherd boy from the land of Canaan, we see a picture of contentment. He was the son of his father's old age, and his absolute favorite. According to scripture, Jacob loved Joseph so much that he made him a tunic, a coat of many colors, to show his adoration and favor of his beloved son. His brothers, obviously older, were seen traveling to neighboring towns and villages working to bring provision for their family. But we do not hear of Joseph traveling with them. Being the preferred son, he unmistakably hung around the family settlement with his father Jacob, soaking in the wisdom, guidance and nurturing of this patriarch. He had no desire to go out with his brothers to hunt, gather and provide for their family, but found his purpose in the bosom of his beloved father.

The Lord's desire for our lives is never small; His will for us is magnificent, and carries with it the height, length, breadth, and width of eternity. The who, what, when, where, and how of our existence are mere conduits designed to get us to the desired destination and ultimate plan of God for our lives. Joseph did not see himself further than the land of Canaan. He could not perceive further than the view in the distance of his brother's silhouettes, as they ventured out of the Valley of Hebron towards Shechem. The only way that God could get him to see further was by quieting his spirit as he lay still in the depths of the night. God invaded his dreams. The Lord revealed His plan for Joseph's life in Genesis 37:5:

"Now Joseph had a dream, and he told it to his brothers; and they hated him even more."

Joseph had no earthly idea what this dream meant. He was just excited to share it with his brothers and his father. Even after the visions in the dreams were revealed, and after his brothers hated him and his father rebuked him, there is no mention of Joseph debating with them or standing up for his individuality or anonymity from this family. He still could not see that God was pushing him towards his destiny. I can remember having dreams since I was a little girl. They were not your ordinary dreams nor were they mere passing visions of the night. I realized much later in my life that God was revealing my purpose to me even before I knew Him. He was showing me, night by night, the prophetic motion-picture of my life, and I am still on that winding reel, as I journey towards my destiny fulfillment.

The Wilderness

God will lead us into our "wilderness" in order to reveal Himself to us. He will thrust us into unwelcomed situations so as to form His character in us. He will allow us to meet certain people, live in certain areas, and work at specific jobs; all in His divine plan. Nothing in this life occurs by happenstance or coincidence. Everything has a purpose and is a piece to the puzzle of your life. Never discount a season as being unimportant or unnecessary; God uses it all! Whether good or bad, He orchestrates each life lesson in symphony with His predestined purpose for you. He holds the keys to your destiny within His grasp. No matter what you see around you; no matter what situations or circumstances you find yourself facing, you must believe that He is working it all together for your good, weaving the fibers of your journey in concert with His blueprint. Even the most devastating experiences along our pathway are utilized by the Father to reveal His glory in and through our lives.

> God will lead us into our "Wilderness" in order to reveal Himself to us.

Joseph's story is overshadowed by multiple instances of tests, trials and yes, tribulation. You would think after the first two to three situations, God would release Joseph into his purpose, his destiny, but this young man was dipped in the fire of affliction. The waters of the deep overwhelmed his existence. The storms of life battered him and abused him. He went from the comfort of his father's arms to the darkest season of his life. His brothers sold him into slavery to the Ishmaelites. The word Ishmaelite means "God hears". Hagar, in the book of Genesis, named her son from Abraham, Ishmael. God heard the cry of Hagar's heart, He heard the cry of Joseph's heart in the pit and therefore, you can rest assured He hears the cries of your heart as well. The Word says, "For He Himself has said, 'I will never leave you nor forsake you.'" Hebrews 13:5b

How could Joseph believe that God was with him through such pain and turmoil? His brothers hated him, conspired to kill him, threw him in a pit and then sold him into slavery. A pit, historically, was found in the middle of the wilderness. It was a test inside of a test. He was separated from his father who loved him dearly, and had no one who cared about him...or did he? In the darkest pits and the coldest wildernesses of our lives, the Lord is always with us. In fact, this is the closest you will ever be to the God of Heaven on this earth. Sound strange? It is in this place of uncertainty, the place of unfamiliar, where God is ever present to reveal Himself to us. Joseph's beginning looked like the scene out of a motion picture film, but we find out that each step along His journey was mapped out by His Heavenly Father. God had a plan, and it was much bigger than Joseph.

Why would God show this tremendous vision to Joseph of him ruling and reigning over a kingdom, walking in power and authority and possessing great wealth and prosperity, and then take him through living hell on earth? God is seen all throughout the Word of God revealing Himself and His promise to His people, and then taking them through great tests, trials and tribulations...their wilderness. God will never push us into our promise without first taking us through our process. He knows what we need in order to walk in full power and authority, without the fleshly desires of pride, arrogance and greed. Our wilderness reveals to us who we really are. It is a time of great training for us, as we look towards the promise God has shown us. God works from the ending of a thing to the beginning. He works out

The Wilderness

all of the details of our lives in the wilderness, preparing us for our promised land.

Through the experiences of the Israelites in exile, we learn that while the Biblical wilderness is a place of danger, temptation and chaos, it is also a place for solitude, nourishment, and revelation from God. In sending the children of Israel out of Egypt towards the Promised Land, God had to take them through the wilderness to break the chains of oppression off of them. He needed to transform their old mindset, in order to bring them into a new way of thinking. They were no longer slaves, but they needed to be trained to see themselves as God saw them. The experience would have only taken them eleven days, but ended up being forty years because they could not see themselves as free; they could not envision a life outside of Egypt. Even when the Lord provided manna and quail in the wilderness in freedom, they complained, and rather desired the leeks, cucumbers and melons of oppression. The Israelites wanted to go back to their old way of life in Egypt.

The Wilderness of Egypt is considered the place of temptation, luxury and ease. Though they were slaves, they found the compromise of sin easier to deal with than the structured obedience and discipline of the wilderness. As children of God, we too are pulled out of the world (Egypt) and placed on our path to our promise through Jesus Christ. How often do we find ourselves wanting to go back, because it just seems too hard to live this life? The role of the wilderness of Egypt was dual in nature. It was considered both a place of refuge and a place of oppression; a place to come up out of, as well as a place to flee to.

"…and was there until the death of Herod, that it might be fulfilled which was spoken by the Lord through the prophet, saying, "**Out of Egypt** I called My Son." Matthew 2:15 (Added Emphasis)

God called His Son "out" of Egypt in this scripture in Matthew, but just two verses earlier, He sent an angel to warn them to "flee to" Egypt.

"Now when they had departed, behold, an angel of the Lord appeared to Joseph in a dream, saying, "Arise, take the young Child and His mother, **flee to Egypt**, and stay there until I bring you word; for Herod will seek the young Child to destroy Him." Matthew 2:13 (Added Emphasis)

There is great instruction that comes in times of chaos and confusion, and as we submit to that 'still small voice' on this inside, we are given specific insight and revelation that will steer us away from danger and toward safety. Though we feel as if no one is with us in this dark place, the Lord is speaking and revealing Himself to us through Holy Spirit. He is our spiritual 'GPS' and if we allow Him to guide our paths and order our footsteps, He will lead us towards our predestined purpose. Through all that Joseph faced along his journey, from the pit to the palace, the Lord was leading Him; He was positioning him for his promise through the preparation of persecution…his wilderness.

I did not understand what God was doing in my life during my initial process. I felt as if I had fallen away from Him and I couldn't hear Him the way I was able to beforehand, but I came to realize through His silence that He needed me to trust Him. He needed me to

The Wilderness

have the confidence in my relationship with Him that He would never leave me or forsake me. This was a time of testing for me. It was a place of preparation where I was being trained to trust totally in His Sovereignty and promise over my life. There are seasons in our lives where the Lord will allow us to face adversity in order to purge us of our fleshly ways. He wants us humble and broken before Him, so He is able to truly use us for His glory. Joseph was his father's favorite son. We don't really sense a tone of pride or arrogance in the scriptures concerning him, but to have a dream that one day his brothers and parents would bow down to him surely could have exposed some sort of haughtiness in this young man's life. I am sure he did not intentionally prance around in his 'coat of many colors' rubbing it in his brother's faces that he was his father's beloved son, but God knows the evil in each of our hearts. We can do *nothing* for the Lord with pride in our hearts. God

> On your path toward your purpose, it is pertinent to recognize you are not the priority.

cannot entrust His plan in the hands of anyone who does not understand that humility is the way up. On your path toward your purpose, it is pertinent to recognize you are not the priority; His will supersedes any selfish motive you can even think to conjure up on your own.

"Or do you not know that your body is the temple of the Holy Spirit who is in you, whom you have from God, and you are not your own? [20] For you were bought at a price; therefore glorify God in your body and in your spirit, which are God's." 1 Corinthians 6:19-20

16

Deborah G. Hunter

All too often, instead of heeding the voice of the Lord, we find ourselves reverting back to our "Egypt's" because the road of transformation seems too difficult for us to endure. We halt, or even stop the ongoing work of Jesus Christ in our lives because we feel life was easier before we got saved. This is truly deception from the enemy of our souls. God has a magnificent plan for your life. He has a promise for you that is beyond your wildest imagination. Don't settle for your past when God has a future of endless possibilities awaiting you.

The story of Joseph gives a much more detailed picture of the Wilderness of Egypt and the ambiguity of its role. Egypt is a place of oppression, as Joseph is initially enslaved, eventually ending up in prison. Egypt is also a place of hope and refuge as Joseph is raised to be second in the land. From this position of great power, he is able to provide a refuge from famine for his family.

Your wilderness is not sent to destroy you; it is allowed so as to provide you with the necessary tools to sustain you during your process, as well as a place where God tests, trains, and releases you to fulfill your destiny! The contrast in roles allows us the opportunity to see God's ultimate love for us. He desires to bless us and increase our capacity to thrive, but it also teaches us to humble ourselves, so that things do not consume us and pull us away from Him.

Egypt also had a reputation as a place of wisdom, and Joseph appeals to this impression by calling on them to find a man "discerning and wise" (Gen 41:33). Of course, Joseph is the man they need, one of the wise, those who know the way the world works in both a divine and a human sense. In the wilderness, God prepares us through exposure to unfamiliar surroundings. When we enter the place of obscurity,

The Wilderness

we don't always see the light at the end of the tunnel. Many times, the darkness of our tests lead us back to the world for answers. We don't always make the right choices, but each mistake we make affords us experience and wisdom for our journey ahead. Joseph was a naïve young man, as seen through the light of his brothers and, I am sure, his father. Being kidnapped by his brothers at such a young age and thrown into a pit, sold as a slave and cast into prison was much for a young boy to endure, but through each experience, God was imparting great wisdom into Joseph's life. He was being *prepared* for his promise.

No matter what battles you are going through, no matter what storms you may be facing; God will use each and every situation to mold and shape you into the man or woman He needs you to be. It is not meant to kill you or destroy you, but it is designed to break you and re-make you. This process will absolutely NOT feel good, but it is necessary in order for you to walk in the predestined purpose of God for your life. You can do this. I am cheering you on!

Chapter Tips

#1: Understand that You Were Created With Purpose in Mind.

You were not just born into this world to exist. You were fashioned by the Creator of the Universe with a plan and a purpose in mind. Every life situation and circumstance makes up the journey you are on called life. Each test, trial & tribulation is a piece to the predestined purpose for your being. You are in the making...

#2: God Knows Your Beginning From Your End

The Bible tells us that we were thought of before we were even formed in our mother's womb. It tells us that God mapped our lives out before He even created us. What encouragement to know that even when I don't know what is going on in my life, He does. Rest in knowing that He will get you to your destiny; trust Him.

#3: The Process is Necessary in Order for You to Reach Your Purpose...Don't Quit!

Just as hard, dirt-encrusted formations are taken through the process of refinement to be revealed as breathtaking gems called diamonds, so are you being formed into the image & likeness of God the Father. It may not feel good

The Wilderness

to be transformed into something you are not accustomed in. Don't despise your process. I see you in your end, and you look like your Daddy!

*"Your Word is a lamp to my feet
and a light to my path."*

Psalm 119:105

Chapter 2

Hunger for the Word

"The Wilderness of Sinai"
(The Place of Truth)

"Your word I have hidden in my heart, that I might
not sin against You."

Psalm 119:11

When I finally made up in my mind that I was going to live wholly
for God and submit my life to Him, I submerged myself in the Word. I
ate, drank and slept meditating on the Holy Scriptures. I could not get
enough of it! I would awaken early in the morning and delve into the
pages of this life-altering, Holy Spirit inspired book. At times, it was
truly my daily bread. I fasted often and threw myself into in depth
study of the Bible. My husband would literally have to take off my

The Wilderness

glasses and peel my Bible and notebook out of my hands in the middle of the night, as I had fallen asleep in deep study. God blessed me tremendously with a job where I was able to work in my own office, allowing me the intimate and personal time to read and write almost incessantly. Not only did I grow healthy in the Word of God, but I was also able to complete my first three books while in this position. It was a time of great intimacy with the Father.

The Word of God is the lifeline of every Believer. It is the ground upon which we stand; the foundation upon which our faith is established. It strengthens, encourages and equips us to live the lives God purposed for us. It provides instruction, guidance, direction and revelation. It is truly the manual to our makeup; the handbook of our destiny. Without constant daily meditation on the Word of God, we are left malnourished and emaciated. Just as we need food to sustain our physical bodies, our spirit requires its sustenance as well. We cannot survive on a bowl of soup for an entire year, so we should not expect last year's Word to provide for us now what it did previously. Joshua 1:8 articulates it best:

"This Book of the Law shall not depart from your mouth, but you shall meditate in it day and night, that you may observe to do according to all that is written in it. For then you will make your way prosperous, and then you will have good success."

The Word of God is living and breathing. It is so complex that one scripture can mean something entirely different for my past, present and future. It crosses time and space, and leaves its imprint on the canvas of our lives, whether we live in Australia or Zimbabwe; whether we lived in second century BC or presently in the 21st century. The

Deborah G. Hunter

Word cannot be contained within the veil of our traditional or religious ideologies. It can reach people of all ages, race, gender, class, culture, economic and social status…it is universal in its approach to mankind. Our souls yearn for ultimate truth in a world so uncertain. Many seek their entire lives for the meaning of life and their existence here on this earth, but never find it. They venture into the depths of religion searching for that which will satisfy the longings of their heart and soul, and settle for that which feels good or sounds good, instead of what IS good, and that is simply the truth of God's Word.

> We refuse the Truth of His Word by craving the benefits while rejecting the process.

The Wilderness of Sinai was a place where God revealed the law to His people. The children of Israel encamped near this mountain after several stops along the way after crossing the Red Sea. It was considered the 'place of Truth'. The Israelites had escaped captivity and journeyed through great seasons of change, as they were stripped daily of the oppression they experienced in Egypt. This was not an easy transition. They had lived their entire lives in slavery. It was all they knew; it was inherent to them. To be enslaved and freed in one day was tremendously overwhelming and perplexing to these men, women and children. The very nature of submission was probably a piercing reminder of the oppression they endured under the rule of Pharaoh. For these people to face a new concept of obedience, it proved to be very challenging. They were elated to be free from the bondage of Egypt and its dictator, but they really struggled in accepting the fact that they now had to submit to Moses and his God.

The Wilderness

How many of us felt and still feel this way when coming to God? Do you remember the day you gave your life to Christ? You knew you needed change in your life, but you battled with whether or not you wanted to give up your 'freedoms'. We desire the peace, joy and blessing that come with being a Christian, but we refuse to lay down our lives and follow Jesus. We refuse the Truth of His Word by craving the benefits while rejecting the process. The wilderness is a place of preparation. The children of Israel had to be reconditioned to living a free life. They had to be trained to discipline themselves and to walk in humility and reverence toward God. The same goes for us. When we are pulled out of the world, we now have to learn to live a new life in Christ Jesus. Our old ways are to fall away through the Truth of His Word concerning us. We must saturate ourselves daily in the water of scripture, so that we drip with the knowledge and wisdom of our Heavenly Father.

"O God, when You went out before Your people, when You marched through the wilderness, Selah. 8The earth shook; the heavens also dropped rain at the presence of God; Sinai itself was moved at the presence of God, the God of Israel. 9You, O God, sent a plentiful rain. Whereby you confirmed Your inheritance, when it was weary. 10Your congregation dwelt in it; You, O God, provided from Your goodness for the poor. 11The Lord gave the WORD; Great was the company of those who proclaimed it…" (Psalm 68:7-11, emphasis mine)

The Word was meant not only to sustain them in the wilderness, but it was to be a foundation upon which they would now live their lives with God. It was not only truth, but it was good. It was and is the moral standard by which we are to reside. This Word should be the utmost priority in our daily lives. The times are revealing the many

Deborah G. Hunter

distractions and hindrances designed to keep us from fellowship in the Word of God. Technology has all but shattered the intimacy not only amongst men, but also with the Lord. We get our daily 'apps' to send us one scripture that is meant to sustain us for the day, but without studying and meditating upon the truths of that Word, we are left to figure it out for ourselves and often, we miss it. We rely upon someone else to feed us the Word of God and take what they say as Truth when we have not examined it ourselves. Deception is very great in the world today, but also in the Church. We know the Word tells us in the last days, deception will grow stronger and people will seek out teachers to tell them what they want to hear, as opposed to the Truth. We need the unadulterated legitimacy of the scriptures if we are to walk in the will of God. We see so many leaders who choose to compromise the integrity of the Word to cater to the outside world's ideals of what we, as Christians, should believe. So it is pertinent to know the Word for yourself! If you are in consistent study and meditation, you will be able to recognize deception when it presents itself to you. We know many will fall away from the faith in these last days; choose not to be one of them.

We are introduced throughout the Word to several men and women of God who were noted for their knowledge and wisdom. Moses is credited to writing the first five books of the Bible, the canons, which are considered the Torah to those of Jewish faith. Though they are seen as the 'law' of scripture, they hold some of the most universal truths and disciplines necessary for our growth and maturity in Christ. The Ten Commandments is probably the most essential aspect of the Christian faith. These guidelines from God are meant to instruct, lead and direct us on the pathway to our purpose. They are tools of morality that shield us from the gross evil of this world. Our Father created us,

The Wilderness

so He knows exactly what we need to successfully maneuver throughout this life and that is wholly in His Word to us. His desire is not to control us, His desire is love. Love covers, love protects. His motive is simple.....LOVE.

Another phenomenal writer of the Bible was David. The Word says he was 'a man after God's own heart' (1 Samuel 13:14) He knew the importance of hiding the Word of God in his heart. He is credited to writing the majority of the book of Psalms. Through the battles and intense struggles of his life, he knew to turn to the scriptures. They were sustenance to his soul, medicine to his mind, bread for his body, and strength for his spirit. David understood that without the Word of God, he could not live; he had nothing without the life-breathing, living expression of God Himself.

> We need the unadulterated legitimacy of the scriptures if we are to walk in the will of God.

Many people in today's Christian circles do not hold the Word of God as a top priority. Some feel that they have enough of the Word on the inside of them to sustain them for the entirety of their lives, while others are falling away from the foundation of Biblical teachings. They have come to the conclusion that it 'doesn't take all of that' to live for God or to go to Heaven, so many have neglected the daily study of God's Word, as well as prayer and fellowship in a church setting. So many believers are struggling in every area of their lives because they abandoned the foundational truths of the Bible. When we forsake daily nourishment in the Word of God, we become weak in mind, body, soul and spirit. The Word says in Mark 12:30:

"And you shall love the Lord your God with all your heart, with all your soul, with all your mind, and with all your strength."

We are not able to love the Lord in this manner if we do not maintain a consistent fellowship with the Holy Spirit inspired Word of God. We say we love Him, but He said if we love Him, we would keep His commandments; His Word. (John14:15) All too often, we feel we have the answers to life and we don't need to read every day or even every week for that matter. As we see aforementioned, it not only nourishes us physically, emotionally, mentally and spiritually, but it also infuses our relationship with our Father. It develops intimacy with the One who created us. It produces a passion and zeal on the inside of us that is undeniable!

When we hide the Word in our hearts, as David so eloquently and passionately stated in the Psalm, we have sustaining power when we enter into life situations that are turbulent and chaotic. God prepares us in the Word for every test, trial and tribulation we may face in this life. His Word is full of wisdom, knowledge, understanding, power, and authority...LIFE!

I remember being thrust into my wilderness and not understanding what was taking place. I could not understand what God was doing, but I had the scriptures ingrained in my heart, they were so deeply rooted that when I felt as if I could not see, hear or feel God, they were all I had. I began to release the Word out of my spirit. I would cry out to the Lord and remind Him of the scriptures in my heart. This provid-

The Wilderness

ed great comfort and strength during some of the darkest times in my life.

The word *ingrained* has several meanings; one meaning is worked into the surface, pores, or fibers of something and very difficult to remove. Another definition is long-established or confirmed in a habit or practice. Both of these are excellent examples of how God wants us to firmly plant the Word of God in our hearts: worked into the surface, pores or fibers of our being and established in habit or practice. When we study the formation of rocks or other solid formations, we see the layers and layers of material mixed throughout the rock. From the years of being formed, particles are embedded deep within the recesses of this formation. This is an allegory that we can relate the Christian life to, and how the Word should be so deeply rooted in our lives that it will be extremely difficult to remove during trying times. The second definition shows us that it should become a habit, or a habitual practice, in our daily lives. Studies say that anything done consistently over a seventeen day period of time automatically becomes a habit. We have to purpose in our hearts to make a daily habit of reading, studying, meditating and searching out the scriptures. We have to hide ourselves within the safety of the pages of this timeless work. Let's look at the Book of John.

> We can no longer scratch the surface of scripture and expect a deeper level of intimacy and anointing from God.

"I am the vine, you are the branches. He who abides in Me, and I in him, bears much fruit; for without Me you can do nothing. [6] If anyone does not abide in Me, he is cast out as a branch and is withered; and they gather them and throw them into the fire, and they are burned. [7] If you abide in Me, and My words abide in you, you will ask what you desire, and it shall be done for you. [8] By this My Father is glorified, that you bear much fruit; so you will be My disciples." (John 15:5-8)

If we abide, or live within the confines of the Word of God, make it our hiding place, then God says we will bear much fruit and we will be considered disciples. We can no longer scratch the surface of scripture and expect a deeper level of intimacy and anointing from God. Surely God is not a microwave God or a drive through window where you can get a blessing in five minutes or less. We have to make this a lifestyle. We should be so consumed by the Word of God that it becomes a part of who we are in our everyday lives. It should be the compass by which our every step is ordered. Every decision, no matter how big or small, should be examined against the scriptures, so we will know what God says about it. So often, we either make hasty decisions based upon our own desires or knowledge, or seek the advice and counsel of someone else before we go to the Lord. Advice and counsel is not bad, in and of itself, but if it does not line up with the Word of God, you must discard it and get to the place that has the answers for your life. God wants us so intimately connected to the Word that we will hear His voice through it. The written Word of God is called the *logos* of the Word. It is the entire content of scripture penned by holy men of God, inspired by Holy Spirit. To delve a little bit deeper, Jesus Himself is considered the Word, or the *Logos*. He is the watermark on the pages of the Bible. He is the meaning behind every word penned on every folio of this Book. Nothing in this Word exists outside of Him. His fingerprint is clearly marked upon it; his

The Wilderness

DNA is intertwined all throughout. We cannot separate Him from the Word; He IS the Word!

"In the beginning was the Word, and the Word was with God, and the Word was God. [2] He was in the beginning with God. [3] All things were made through Him, and without Him nothing was made that was made." (John 1:1-3)

The answers to our life are found in Jesus, the Word. His character, His nature, His Spirit is what we are striving to emulate. We want to be found looking like Him, acting like Him, speaking like Him, walking like Him…living like Jesus. But that can only happen when we submerge our hearts in the Word of God. We have the greatest example to go before us. Though He is the Word, Jesus Himself, as He lived in His fleshly body was found studying the scriptures at a very young age. Why would He have to do this if He was considered the Word? What need would He have to read something He already was? Though He was God in the flesh, He still had to deal with His natural existence on this earth. He was still required to walk out the laws of this realm in His earthly body. The Bible said He was found in the temple with the scholars rehearsing the scriptures. The wisdom and insight this young man possessed astonished those of more astute character, experience and religious acumen. They sat speechless as Jesus' understanding and answers to the Word well exceeded his twelve years on this earth. If our Lord had to submerge Himself in the scriptures, how much more should we? It is a lifestyle of reading, studying and meditating that prepares us for the tests, trials and tribulation we will face on our journey. He was being prepared for His wilderness here on earth.

Deborah G. Hunter

We see from scripture He stayed behind in Jerusalem as His father, mother and family began the journey back home. Though His Spirit was yearning for the Word and time in the presence of those with great wisdom, Jesus neglected His earthly headship. Though He was God in the flesh, He was still obligated to fulfill His earthly responsibilities; one being obedience. As Mary and Joseph had traveled a day's journey, they realized their son was not in the company with them. They immediately ventured back towards Jerusalem in search of Him. After three days, they finally found Him in the temple. Their response was one in which is very normal for any parent whose child has taken it upon themselves to do their own will. Let's take a look:

"So when they saw Him, they were amazed; and His mother said to Him, "Son, why have You done this to us? Look, Your father and I have sought you anxiously." (Luke 2:48)

They were genuinely concerned, as well as upset He took it upon Himself at the age of twelve to stay behind without His family and amongst people He did not know. I know I would be extremely upset if any of my children decided to do what Jesus did; it is just parental instinct to want to protect your children. Jesus' response was bold, at best, in light of the fact He was in disobedience to His earthly parents.

"And He said to them, "Why did you seek Me? Did you not know that I must be about My Father's business?"

Now, if any one of my children chose to speak this way to me or their father, it would surely have consequences behind it, as it should. The next verse reveals God's order and direction for us all. "Then He

The Wilderness

went down with them and came to Nazareth, and was subject to them, but His mother kept all these things in her heart."

Though He was God, He still had to obey earthly headship; He cannot defy the principles of earth, just because He is God. God will not go against Himself; His Word. Jesus had to face the consequences of His disobedience to His parents. This was part of His preparation.

"though He was a Son, yet He learned obedience by the things which He suffered." (Hebrews 5:8)

So must we all learn obedience to God, as we journey towards our Promised Land. We are being formed into His image and likeness.

> Though He was God, He still had to obey earthly headship; He cannot defy the principles of earth, just because He is God.

From the age of twelve to thirty-three, Jesus was being groomed for his assignment. We do not hear of any real battles concerning Him until He is released into ministry at the age of thirty-three. It goes without saying that if He was found in the temple at the age of twelve with the scholars studying and meditating upon the Word, then we are to assume He continued in the scriptures and prayer throughout His adolescence and young adulthood. It was absolutely a necessary part of His process of preparation for His promise. He still battled with the flesh, and had to be taught and trained to walk according to God's will, in order to fulfill His work on this earth. We cannot skip the process, and we MUST keep the Word of God at the center of it all.

Deborah G. Hunter

We see the blatant disobedience acted out by the children of Israel after they were led out of Egypt. Their first stop after passing over dry land through the Red Sea was the 'Wilderness of Sin'. They had been under this oppressive regime their entire lives, and though they were beaten into submission and obedience, their minds were the furthest from outright obeisance to their masters. Their hatred and contempt for years of slavery kept the Israelites in a constant state of rage and rebellion. Any chance they could get to 'go against the grain' they took, but not without cost or consequence. When they finally had their chance at freedom, true autonomy, they did not know how to receive it. They rebelled, murmured, and complained at every juncture. Though God was supplying manna in the wilderness, it was not enough for them. The daily 'bread' they were receiving became stale to them and therefore, they desired to return back to Egypt, bondage, because they felt they would be fed better there. They were willing to give up their freedom, their Promised Land, to go back to what was comfortable, or what fed their fleshly needs, instead of the Bread of Life which would sustain them spirit, soul, mind, and body.

Don't think for one moment that the world has anything to offer you now that you are in Christ. When you hunger and thirst after Him and His righteousness, He will fill you to overflowing. You will be satisfied with His daily bread and another's you will not covet, or crave. This is the place God desires for you; to be so content with His Word and His ways that you will be transformed into His image. God leads us into the wilderness to cause us to depend wholly upon Him and Him alone. This is a place of intimacy unlike any other. It is just you and God, walking through the dry places of your past and being watered by the Word on the inside of you. You are shedding your old

The Wilderness

ways and clothing yourself in the newness of your relationship with the Lord.

I remember so clearly this time in my 'wilderness'. I felt as if the Word of God was stripped from my life? I could not understand what was happening to me, and at one point, I thought I had actually lost my salvation. I thought I had done something so wrong against God that He removed Himself from my life, that He left me. This was not Biblical, as the Word says, "He will never leave us or forsake us." (Deuteronomy 31:6) But it felt as if He had surely left me. I was on my 'own' in this dry place to seek out what was inside of me. The years and years of feeding my heart the scriptures were not in vain. It would prove absolutely pertinent to my journey through my wilderness. I had to encourage myself in the Word, as David did. If I had not known the Word of God, I could have spent many years wandering in this place, but this is not God's intent or purpose for the wilderness. The wilderness is not your destiny; it is a doorway to your Promised Land! Keep the Word close, ever before you, so you can allow it to lead you out of this season and into the next.

The Bible says that there will come a time when this Word has to be so hidden within our hearts because of the lack of its release within the earth. Don't take it for granted, as it may not be with us much longer. Many nations around the world are banning the Bible and not allowing any type of Bible fellowship in churches or home settings, but some are sacrificing their lives daily just to read this precious Word that many in the Western world take for granted.

Deborah G. Hunter

"Behold, the days are coming," says the Lord God, "That I will send a famine on the land, Not a famine of bread, Nor a thirst for water, But of hearing the words of the Lord." (Amos 8:11)

We must allow the process of His Word to transform us and prepare us for all He has in store for us. Our Father knows what we need and He knows the exact time and season in our lives when we can receive, with maturity, the things He has prepared for us. Be patient and endure till the end. Keep His Word as your unyielding foundation and He will lead you in the paths He has preordained for you.

> The wilderness is not your destiny; it is a doorway to your Promised Land!

Chapter Tips

#4: The Word of God is the only real thing that will sustain you in your wilderness.

God sends us into the wilderness in order for us to grow and mature in His ways. He extracts the old ways of thinking and impregnates us with the living Word of God, which is able to keep us from stumbling and falling. It is our life-sustaining bread; we cannot live without the Word of God!

#5: Hide the Word in your heart.

Tests and trials are sure to come. As you hide the Word of God in your heart, when hard times approach, they will spring forth like wells full of water in declaration to your atmosphere. Speak the Word and watch your situation change!

#6: The logos versus the rhema of God's Word.

As you commit to a lifestyle of reading, studying, and meditating upon the written (logos) Word, you will begin to hear His voice (rhema). I don't know about you, but I need to hear my Father's voice!

The Wilderness

#7: God cannot go against His Word; Jesus is the embodiment of Scripture.

The Bible says, "though He was a Son, yet He learned obedience by the things which He suffered." (Hebrews 5:8) Everyone must go through their own process of preparation if we are to reach our destiny; our Promise. Jesus is no different than you and me on earth. He had to submit, and so must we. Obedience is a crucial aspect of our growth and maturity, and must be practiced at all times. The wilderness is a place where obedience is tried and tested. Come out with your card stamped, "Passed!"

"I have found David the son of Jesse, a man after My own heart, who will do all My will."

Acts 13:22b

Chapter 3

A Servant's Heart

"The Wilderness of Ziph"
(The Place of Anointing)

"The Lord has sought for Himself a man after His own heart...."

1 Samuel 13:14a

God's intent for man, in the beginning, was to have a people whom He could walk with, talk with and commune with on a daily basis; free from obstruction and separation. His heart longed to fellowship with His creation uninterrupted in the cool of the day, as they walked side by side in the Garden. Adam was the man created after God's heart; in His image and in His likeness. Nothing blocked the flow between Creator and creation, until the man disobeyed God and ate of the tree forbidden by Him; the tree of the knowledge of good and evil. Adam possessed all wisdom. He was given authority over all

The Wilderness

the creatures on earth, naming the entirety of them. Why would he need or want anything else? He had it all.

Many times, though God has given us all we desire, we somehow find ourselves seeking more. We saw the children of Israel delivered from the hand of Pharaoh and carried towards their Promised Land, only to find themselves complaining that they wanted to go back to the 'familiar' because it seemed better than where they were going. Their deliverer, Moses, had it all as most viewed it, but there was something missing. As he learned of his true identity as a Hebrew, compassion swelled in his heart for his people. In an effort to come to the rescue of one of his people being beaten by an Egyptian soldier, Moses found himself back on the other side of the tracks. He could not face who he had become, so he fled to the desert to escape the torment of his mind. Deserts are very dry places, very similar to that of a wilderness. It is in these 'dry places' where God strips us of all that is "us" and begins to form in us a heart that seeks to put others first; a heart to serve. After his season of purging in his 'wilderness', Moses came out with the heart of a servant. He emerged with the single-minded focus of freeing his people from the strong-arm of Pharaoh. His desire was not the kingdom he had forfeited and all of the riches he attained growing up as the son of the wealthiest man in Egypt, but he lay it all down to serve his God and his people. His selfless act of love revealed much about the man named Moses. It can be likened to that of our Lord and Savior, Jesus Christ who lay down his very life that we may live eternally with Him in Heaven. A true servant of God. What love!

When we turn our lives over to the Lord, we are no longer our own. We trade our former lives for the new life we have been given in

Deborah G. Hunter

Christ Jesus. We are to lay down not only our lives, but our will; the desire to do as we choose, and to think only of ourselves and what we need and want. Our hearts, as we begin to read the Word of God, are transformed and our minds are renewed to think like Jesus, and eventually, our lives should reflect and display the living Word of God.

"And do not be conformed to this world, but be transformed by the renewing of your mind, that you may prove what is that good and acceptable and perfect will of God." Romans 12:2

> True fulfillment in life will only come through total surrender to the Father, the Creator of the Universe.

I placed my life in the Father's hands very early on in my walk with Him. I am not quite sure why it happened so quickly, but I endured so much at a young age that the true, agape love of God captured my heart and I totally surrendered to the Lord. God began to reveal His heart to me and placed it in me. My love for Him and for people began to skyrocket! His desires became my desires; it was no longer about me, but about His perfect will working in and through me. This is God's ultimate plan for us all; to live and move through each of us to reach a lost and dying world. Are you willing to lay it all down for Him and for others? Are you willing to endure your 'wilderness' in order to fulfill His plan for your life? True fulfillment in life will only come through total surrender to the Father, the Creator of the Universe. His desire is for each of us to walk in His image and likeness and to bear His very nature. This can only happen through transformation…our 'wilderness'.

The Wilderness

One man referred to as the 'man after God's own heart', David, the son of Jesse the Bethlehemite, is the epitome of servant hood in the Word of God. David came on the scene in 1 Samuel Chapter 16 tending to his father's flock, a shepherd boy who had a heart for his sheep. He counted it not robbery to serve his father in this manner; he was truly a man after God's own heart. As David began to mature, he was sought after by the Spirit of God.

"And Samuel said to Jesse, "Are all the young men here?" Then he said, "There remains yet the youngest, and there he is, keeping the "sheep." And Samuel said to Jesse, "Send and bring him, For we will not sit down till he comes here." (1 Samuel 16:11)

When you are "found" serving, the Lord will seek you out for His purposes. David was not looking for recognition, he was serving faithfully because he had a 'servant's heart'. As he began to serve Saul, the king, the Lord began to reveal more and more the character, loyalty and obedience of this young shepherd boy. He had the favor of God resting upon his life, and it was revealed in every aspect of it. He not only went to war and defeated all of the armies that came up against him, but he also, in downtime from war, served Saul by playing the harp to quiet his spirit. The Word of God tells us that each time a distressing spirit of the Lord came upon Saul, he would call for David to play the harp...a 'servant's heart'. After a season, David began to be recognized not only by the men he went to war with, but also the women in the camps who began to sing songs in honor of his victories.

"So the women sang as they danced, and said: 'Saul has slain his thousands, And David his ten thousands." 8 Then Saul was very angry, and the saying displeased him; and he said, "They have ascribed to David ten thousands, and to me they have ascribed only thousands. Now what more can he have but the kingdom?" 9 "So Saul eyed David from that day forward." (1 Samuel 18:7-9)

No matter how angry Saul became toward David, he continued to serve his master with loyalty and respect. Saul thrust spear after spear in his direction, but each time, David escaped. Saul was very afraid of him because the Lord was with David, but this did not hinder Saul from continuing to try to kill this faithful servant. But each time, David kept his composure and continued to serve this man that hated him and faithfully pursued his destiny. What kind of man was this? What man would stand by peacefully and allow someone to boldly attempt to kill him? What manner of man would persist with love, compassion, loyalty and service in the face of hatred? We see the shadow, or type, of Jesus Christ in the life of the servant David. It is no wonder we see our Lord and Savior descending from the lineage of David, a humble servant who lay down his life to serve others with humility and reverence.

"And David behaved wisely in all his ways, and the Lord was with him." (1 Samuel 18:14)

How often do we find ourselves desiring to avenge ourselves before those who attack us for no apparent reason? Time and time again, we see many who find it necessary to speak up and let everyone know they are innocent, and the adversity coming up against them is unfounded. This is reasonable, right? Well, in the Word of God, we see frequently where the Lord says otherwise. The Bible admonishes us to endure every temptation and to refrain from worry, complaining

The Wilderness

and seeking out justice from those who wrongly accuse us. In fact, the Word tells us to literally, "Turn the other cheek." (Luke 6:29) In other words, let them accuse; let them persecute you.

"Remember the word that I said unto you, The servant is not greater than his lord. If they have persecuted me, they will also persecute you..." (John 15:20a)

I went through a season very similar to that of the patriarch David. My wilderness proved to be a time of great testing and growth. I cannot say I took the noble road this servant did; I wanted to shout on the rooftops that I was being wrongfully treated and lied upon. I went above and beyond, seeking to vindicate myself and found that no one was listening. I realized I was hurting myself even the more as I sought to obtain justice for the persecution I was facing. God immediately rebuked me, and commanded me to endure. He summoned me to humble myself and to continue walking in honesty, integrity and yes, submission to His will for my life. I did not understand at the time what the Lord was doing, but as I look back now, He was preparing me in the vestibule of my wilderness. This was the entranceway toward holiness in Christ Jesus. Our Lord kept his mouth closed as he endured hatred and lies from those who were supposed to be of religious hierarchy. Jesus continued to serve those around him, even through the pain and parody of persecution...a servant's heart.

This was truly one of the most difficult things I had to learn as God took me through my wilderness. I have always loved hard and served those around me, but this season proved to be very challenging for me. I was talked about, lied upon, used, mocked and outright ignored in some instances from those I considered my brothers and

48

Deborah G. Hunter

sisters in Christ. It was devastating to say the least. I just wanted to run as far away as I could, but the Lord commanded me to submit and to serve without hesitation. These were His words to me, "You will humble yourself and serve faithfully in this house until I release you. You will sit where I tell you to sit and you will lift your hands in worship and adoration of me in the midst of this persecution. You will fast, pray, cover and intercede for those who are using you and lying about you, and you will love them as I have loved you." This was absolutely the most loving yet difficult correction I had ever received; this was a shift in my life that opened up my eyes to true servant hood and humility. I knew this was not about me, but ultimately, for God's purposes. I learned

> Jesus continued to serve those around him, even through the pain and parody of persecution…a servant's heart.

to truly LIVE the Word of God, not just speak it. I began to love my enemies, to pray for those who persecuted me and intentionally used me, and blessed those whose only desire was to curse me. My flesh was slowly being peeled away and the Lord was building up my spiritual muscles.

This is how David was able to operate in pure power and authority, through his submission and obedience to the Lord in the midst of his wilderness. The most noted wilderness we hear in the story of David is the "Wilderness of Ziph," which translates "flowing" or the 'place of anointing'. Though he was facing death nearly every day, David had the Spirit of the Lord upon his life. Because of his humility, submission and obedience, David had an undeniable anointing overflowing through him. At each interval, David made a vow not

The Wilderness

to touch his king, his leader. He promised he would never lay a hand upon Saul.

""David stayed in the wilderness in the strongholds, and remained in the hill country in the wilderness of Ziph. And Saul sought him every day, but God did not deliver him into his hand." 1 Samuel 23:14

How often do we feel like "overtaking" our enemies? More often than not, our flesh takes over and our first instinct is to shout to the heavens that the treatment we are receiving is unfair, or we are completely innocent of the verbal attacks by others. How often are we quick to avenge ourselves, instead of allowing the glory of God to trump our temporary feelings of frustration? The heart of a true servant submits his/her feelings to the Lord and puts His will above their own. A submitted child of God wants His purpose to manifest through them, no matter what persecution may arise against them. As we grow in Christ, His will becomes our will, His plans become our plans and His heart becomes our heart. At this point in our walk with God, we should be allowing the will of God to override any and all selfless ideas of retribution. Learn of His ways and study His Word, so you can align yourself with His promise over your life.

"Make Your face shine upon Your servant, And teach me Your statutes."Psalm 119:35

God summoned me time and again to keep my mouth shut and my hands clean of confusion. It was not easy, and I wish I could tell you I passed every test, but I definitely failed a few. I learned a lot about the Lord and about myself during this time. I have grown so much since then, and have begun to pass a few of my tests. I have

Deborah G. Hunter

learned that much of what I have gone through was not an attack of the enemy, but redirection from the Lord; a process of training, or preparation, for the promise over my life. I stopped rebuking what God Himself was sending to produce transformation in me. My entire thought process shifted from victim to victor. It was no more, "God, why is this happening to me?" but now, "Father, who and what is this for?" This was a crucial turning point for me, and I pray as you continue to read you, too, will come to a place of submission in your walk with the Lord.

David's life dripped with submission to the Lord and His will. He had so many reasons to disobey God and harm Saul, but he refused. David understood not only the principle of loyalty and obedience, but he also knew God's Word, "Touch not my anointed and do my prophets no harm." (1 Chronicles 16:22) Saul was anointed king by God and at one point, walking in the will of God for his life. Though he strayed off of this track, David knew it was not his place or his timing to remove Saul from his throne, but solely the Lord's. David recognized he needed to endure his 'process' until it was time for God to release him.

How many of us begin our wilderness journey and because we commence to endure trials and temptations, seek to blame others, satan and even God, and release ourselves from the work of God in our lives? Instead of going around in circles, choose to remain surrendered and submitted to the process of preparation in your wilderness. All too often, we succumb to the temptation of promotion and cut off the necessary work of God in our lives intended to produce growth, integrity and maturity. We seek titles, positions, fortune and fame, and end up in a place of loneliness and depression. Things and status

The Wilderness

cannot and will not fill the void in our lives where only God can reside. When we allow His perfect work to be operative in us, He gives us a heart to serve, as opposed to being served.

David knew the call of God upon his life, but he also knew there was a set time to be released in his calling. He refused to step out of the will of God and hinder the process of preparation needed to position him for his promise. Be the kind of servant God can use, as David was. Purpose to allow the Lord to mold you and shape you, through His Word, to be effective in the place He has prepared for you. Lay down your need to rush into situations that could ultimately lead to your destruction. David, though he was called, would have harmed so many people if he had taken it upon himself to kill Saul. He would have cut himself off from the promise if he had not obeyed the Lord. His remarkable character and undeniable loyalty to King Saul provided credibility to the call of God upon his life. He endured great persecution and personal struggle, but he passed his test. David, as he served his king faithfully, was being placed in position for his destiny.

There was a point during my wilderness journey where I just wanted to run. Nothing was making sense, and my heart was growing weary, but the Lord was with me. He never left me alone, and He provided everything I needed, as I cried out to Him. This space in time along my journey drew me closer to my Father than any other season. I had no choice but to depend upon Him, solely. My tears turned to joy, as I began to understand what He was doing in my life. I started to accept His process in me and I learned to trust Him in ways I never imagined.

Deborah G. Hunter

Understand that God sees every deed and service you render to Him and toward His people. Your total surrender to Him will prove to be the most significant decision you will ever make in your life. It is the 'mark' of a servant...it is a trait of a son.

Chapter Tips

#8: To be used by God, you must possess the heart of a servant.

From Moses, to David, to Jesus, we see a pattern of humility, brokenness, surrender, and sacrifice in the lives of these men who made a huge impact in this world for God. It is crucial to let the Lord prepare you for the purpose on your life. In skipping this process, you will not only harm yourself, but you can hurt so many others along the journey. Let Him produce a perfect work within your heart.

#9: Character, loyalty and obedience are key in servant hood.

So many people know what they are called to do, but refuse to be taught and trained not only by the Word of God, but by those who God sets over their lives to train them. In the vestibule of the wilderness, these traits are learned and subsequently 'lived out' in our journey in Christ. Be sure you don't do anything for God without them.

#10: Persecution is one of the greatest tests in the life of a true servant of God.

Can you serve unhindered in the lives of those who are persecuting you? Will you possess a "heart like David" in the midst of great pain, parody, and persecution? Can you pray for your enemies, bless those who curse you, and

The Wilderness

still love those who spitefully use you? If you cannot answer yes to any of these questions, you have not weathered your wilderness, and need to go back and allow the Lord to transform your life for His glory.

"The woman said to Him, "Sir, You have nothing to draw with, and the well is deep. Where then do You get that living water?

John 4:11

Chapter 4

Drenched

"The Wilderness of En Ge'di"
(The Place of Living Water)

"He who believes in Me, as the Scripture has said, out of his heart
will flow rivers of living water."

John 7:38

Throughout our lives, we will experience many ups and downs.
Even as Believers in Jesus Christ, we are not exempt from the trials of
life. In fact, these trials are what form Christ-like character in us. We
found out in the previous chapters that we are commissioned to go
through each process God has planned for us, in order to fulfill His
promise over our lives. From purpose being planted inside of us, to the
Truth of God's Word ingrained in our hearts, we are led into the arms

The Wilderness

of our Father, and our hearts are replaced with His; the heart of a servant. Serving others, especially those who seem ungrateful or even unlovable, is not an easy thing to do. Our flesh will rise up in opposition if we are not covered on a daily basis. Jesus is truly our perfect example. He was not a man that did not experience all that we have in this world, and He, too, went through each process we have had to. He understood the necessity of preparation and all that was required of him during each season.

The Word reveals to us, step by step, the road Jesus walked towards His ultimate purpose in life. Through every twist and turn, we see God perfecting His walk and revealing Himself through each test and trial. From His proclamation into this world to His death on the cross, Jesus endured some very dry places along His journey. God never leaves us without provision to carry out His purpose. The Word says, "And my God shall supply all your need according to His riches in glory by Christ Jesus." (Philippians 4:19) God allowed every need to be met along the pathway to His purpose. God will line up every assignment in the time it is meant to come to pass. He will order our footsteps, divinely, so that we reach our destination in His perfect timing. The Word in Matthew Chapter three reveals to us the initial release of Jesus into the conduit of His Father's plan for His life on earth.

"In those days John the Baptist came preaching in the wilderness of Judea, 2 And saying, "Repent, for the kingdom of heaven is at hand!" 3 For this is he who was spoken of by the prophet Isaiah, saying: "The voice of one crying in the wilderness: 'Prepare the way of the Lord; Make His paths straight.'" (Matthew 3:1-3)

Deborah G. Hunter

John proclaims the entrance of the true and "Living Water," and prepares the people to get ready to go to a higher level; one he could not provide for them. There are seasons in our lives where we think we are "good" or that we have arrived, and experienced enough of God that we don't need a daily filling up of His Spirit. This could not be more wrong. John told the people that he would baptize with water unto repentance, but there was another coming who would baptize them with the Holy Spirit and fire. They needed more to sustain them during their wilderness seasons. We spoke earlier of the absolute need to hide the Word of God in our hearts, but it is just as pertinent to stay filled with the precious Holy Spirit of God. The Word of God will keep us grounded, but Holy Spirit will confirm to us that we are in the right place, at the right time, doing the right thing. Holy Spirit is our spiritual "GPS," leading, directing, and guiding us towards our purpose.

"When He had been baptized, Jesus came up immediately from the water; and behold, the heavens were opened to Him, and He saw the Spirit of God descending upon Him. 17 And suddenly a voice came from heaven, saying, "This is My beloved Son, in whom I am well pleased." (Matthew 3:16-17)

Our Lord had been "drenched" in the waters of baptism and emerged with the proclamation of a son, the Son of God. His obedience brought about the blessing of God over His life. God was pleased with this act of submission and faithfully rewarded Jesus with public approval. All too often, we expect God to elevate us without the process of preparation in our lives. We desire the title or position without the character development and lessons of integrity learned in our "wilderness". God desires that none of us would fall, but if we

The Wilderness

refuse the process, we are destined for destruction. Jesus understood the course He had to take and did so with utmost honor and integrity.

After giving my life back to the Lord, I catapulted in the Word of God. I submerged myself into scripture and studied almost incessantly. I read commentaries and purchased every kind of resource I possibly could that would help me to know more about God, from Bible dictionaries to Bible Concordances. I studied the lives of each person in the Word and read historical books on each of them. I drenched myself in Bible teachings from some of the most influential

> Holy Spirit is our spiritual "GPS," leading, directing, and guiding us towards our purpose.

preachers of the past and present. The Word was constantly before my face or in my ears. I became relentless in my pursuit of the scriptures. My knowledge of the Bible grew extensively, yet there was still some sort of void in my life. I was not filled with the Holy Spirit. I knew of the gift, and saw many others receive it, but never experienced this for myself. I made the choice that I wanted more of God; I desired a deeper level of intimacy with the Lord, so I asked God to fill me with His precious Holy Spirit.

From the moment of infilling, my life began to change. Though I knew the Word, I was now hearing God speak to my spirit. I began to hear instruction and direction for my life; my marriage, my children, my finances and my business. I was now receiving specific plans to carry out my purpose. This also ushered in a season of great prophecy over my life. The Lord was sending people to prophesy His will for

Deborah G. Hunter

me, just as John proclaimed the coming of Jesus, the Living Water...the Son of God. So, we must understand how important this process of being "drenched," or filled, with the Holy Spirit is in the life of every Believer. It unlocks a door to our destiny, and propels us to go deeper in relationship with our Father God. He not only wants us to know "of" Him, but He also wants to speak to us, Father to child. He desires relationship with His children.

Many never experience this next level in their walk with God due to fear, or just out of unbelief. There are several church denominations that do not believe in the infilling of Holy Spirit. They see it as weird or "cultic," and dismiss this crucial component of the Godhead. So many Christians are living a defeated life, because they choose to neglect this pertinent part of their process. They know the Word, but aren't trained to hear the voice of their spirit. They have head knowledge, but no heart knowledge. Most see God as a dictator, as opposed to a Father. The Bible says, "The letter kills, but the Spirit gives life." (2 Corinthians 3:6) If we read the Word only without the Spirit revealing the heart of God, then we will never see God for who He really is to us. So many use the Word of God as a means to suppress and oppress the people of God. They take the law of the Word and beat people down, instead of building them up and providing them with the life-sustaining "Living Water" of God.

Again, if you are not in relationship with God, you will never know what it means to be loved; therefore, you will not know how to love others. The heart of a servant will dissolve if it is not kept fluid through the consistent infilling of Holy Spirit. It must be "drenched" to wash away any residue of our flesh and selfish agendas.

The Wilderness

In I Samuel, we see the servant David running for his life from King Saul. David was in constant flight, as his master grew colder and colder by the day. As he fled, he entered into the Wilderness of En Ge'di, or the place of "Living Water". This area of the Judean desert was barren, except for certain areas that housed springs, or fountains, of water. En Ge'di also means *spring of the kid* or *fountain of the goat*. These were areas where shepherds would lead their flocks to drink from the ravines, while traveling through the dry deserts. David found a place of refreshing in the Wilderness of En Ge'di. He was tired and drained from the constant running from Saul, but found solace in the midst of his dry place.

"Now it happened when Saul had returned from following the Philistines, that it was told him, saying, 'Take note! David is in the Wilderness of En Ge'di.'" (1 Samuel 24:1)

In times of great distress or confusion, where you run is very important. Don't revert back to your past, but run head on towards your future. "...looking unto Jesus, the author and finisher of our faith." (Hebrews 12:2) Run to the water, the "Living Water," who is able to refresh and replenish you, soul and spirit. Be sure to take time out to refresh yourself. You cannot continue to run this race on fumes. God sees exactly where you are in your wilderness and is ready to replenish and refresh you where you are. Stop trying to be the superhero of faith. If Jesus had to be "drenched" in the waters of refreshing, so too must we. God was preparing Him for what He was about to face in His wilderness.

We see another example of God's faithfulness and willingness to pour out refreshing in the life of a woman who was ostracized and

Deborah G. Hunter

belittled by those in her community. We meet the Samaritan woman in the book of John chapter four. Jesus, extremely tired from His journey, takes a very strange course, off the path He and His disciples intended on journeying to get a drink of water. The distance from Judea to Galilee was approximately fifty miles. The time it would take Jesus to get to Galilee by passing through Samaria would add another twenty miles onto their journey. Surely, there were springs and ravines closer where He could have stopped to be refreshed? What took our Lord into the city of Samaria, a place considered "unclean" by Jews? This would be considered the last place they would ever go for drinking water.

"But He needed to go through Samaria." (John 4:4)

Jesus was being led by the Spirit of God to this place. He sat by the well, Jacob's well, when a woman approached to draw water. The Word says it was the sixth hour, meaning about noon day. Most women ventured out very early in the morning to draw water for their families to cook and to clean. So why was this woman drawing water at noon, and obviously alone? Jesus said to her, "Give me a drink?" Astonished, the woman rebutted asking Him why He, a Jew, would ask her, a Samaritan, for water, as Jews did not deal with Samaritans.

"Jesus answered and said to her, "If you knew the gift of God, and who it is who says to you, 'Give me a drink,' you would have asked Him, and He would have given you living water." (John 4:10)

The Samaritan woman was perplexed. She had no idea who this man was and how He could think He was able to offer her something that even her forefather Jacob could not. He had nothing to draw the water with, so how was He going to provide this "living water"?

The Wilderness

How often do we doubt God and His promises of provision for us? We know His Word like the back of our hand, but somehow, we don't trust that He will do exactly what He says He will do. This woman "knew" of the coming Messiah, but she had no relationship with Him. She had no discernment to know she was standing in the midst of the Son of God. The Spirit of God is a revealer. He shows us, or reveals to us, things we may normally not see with our natural eyes. He came not only to show her who she was, but to reveal to her who He was.

> This woman "knew" of the coming Messiah, but she had no relationship with Him.

In our wilderness seasons, God desires to reveal to us more of Himself. He leads us into dry places to strip us of ourselves and to build up our spirits in Him. He desires to strengthen us during these times to prepare us for elevation, and the tests and trials that come with it. Jesus wanted the Samaritan woman to see herself as He saw her. He needed her to see further than her current circumstances and life situations. He required her to be honest with herself, as well as with Him. In order for you to go to the next level, you must learn that honesty and integrity are key to keeping you grounded in your Promised Land. You must be able to face the "man in the mirror".

The Samaritan woman thought this was just another ordinary day of going to the well and drawing water, but she encountered the "Living Water" of Jesus Christ and was drenched in His love and compassion. Her hour of retrieving water was no coincidence. She was an outcast among outcasts. This woman was cut off from the fellow-

66

Deborah G. Hunter

ship of her fellow Samaritans due to her "seemingly risky" lifestyle. She was married many times, and was now living with a man who was not her husband. She risked great embarrassment and condemnation from her community, especially the women who met at this well early every morning, so she waited until no one was there to draw her water. How empty she must have felt? She was in a very dry place...her wilderness. God came to meet her and to reveal to her that she would no longer thirst again after encountering the "Living Water". Her dry place became a spring of life, replenishing and reviving areas of her life that she, and many others, assumed were dead. This woman's life became drenched in the love of God, a love she had never before experienced.

God desires that we experience His agape love, a love that no one else is able to offer. He wants us to know Him as Father, and to live daily in His presence. Without constant communion with the Lord, we are left to the vices of this world and they eventually suck us dry of any life that is in us. The Living Water of the Word and of His Spirit supplies a continuous river of faith, hope, and love. We are promised to never lack for anything, as we seek His presence and trust in Him. It is in our wildernesses where on dependency upon everything and everyone is cut off and the umbilical cord of life is attached to our Creator, our Father.

In each of these Biblical accounts, we see God passionately pursuing His people, desiring that they would trust in Him and Him alone. He reveals Himself as the sustainer of life, the "Living Water" each of them needed to make it through their dry place, or wilderness. He is a jealous God. He will share His glory with no one. When we put our focus on others, either to get us out of situations or giving them

The Wilderness

power over us to hold us in bondage, we grieve His heart. When we refuse the process of our wilderness, we are left in desolation and there is no relief. Our attempts at refreshing end up useless.

"For My people have committed two evils: They have forsaken Me, the fountain of living waters, And hewn themselves cisterns—broken cisterns that can hold no water." (Jeremiah 2:13)

The woman of Samaria came every day to the well of her forefather Jacob. Daily she drew water from a source that could not quench her thirst. Her "cistern" was broken. No matter how much she tried to fill it with the love of man, it could not satisfy the longing of her soul for real love. She became emptier by the day, to the point that marriage was no longer sacred to her. Her trust in man had become so tainted that she decided to settle for whatever she could find; whoever would take her in and give her some sort of intimacy. Don't lose your identity in others, or allow their words to create your reality.

No matter what you have done and no matter what circumstances have arisen in your life, know that God is able to quench every fiery dart of the enemy and every judgmental tongue of your accusers. They don't hold one key to the gates of hell; neither do they have a position at the throne of Heaven to throw you in or keep you out. Trust in the Lord your God and He will fill every parched place of your existence. He comes to give us life and life more abundantly. The Samaritan woman held onto the last hope of legacy she had, the well of her forefather Jacob. She "identified" herself as an heir of this patriarch, and this was most likely the only place of solitude she found in the midst of judgment and condemnation, but it was still not enough.

Deborah G. Hunter

"Jesus answered and said to her, "Whoever drinks of this water will thirst again." 14 "but whoever drinks of the water that I shall give him will never thirst. But the water that I shall give him will become in him a fountain of water springing up into everlasting life." (John 4:13-14)

> Jesus not only confronted the Samaritan woman with love, but also with Truth.

Jesus not only confronted the Samaritan woman with love, but also with Truth. He requires us to get real with ourselves and real with Him. If we continue to remain stuck in the ways of this world, we will never find true fulfillment. But when we allow the process of preparation in our wilderness to have its perfect work, we are then introduced to the "Living Water", Jesus Christ. He comes in when we let go, when we surrender totally to His light, the Truth revealed to us.

The woman at the Well did not "see" who He was until she was confronted with the truth about herself. God loves us so much that He will not leave us in our mess; He wants us free. He desires the best for our lives and will go out of His way to meet us at our "well". When He finds you, allow His "Living Water" to spring up in your life. Let His Truth wash you and free you from the desolation of your wilderness. Allow His Spirit to fill every barren place in your life. Surrender to His will and seek His purpose for you. Your wilderness is not punishment; it is the process of preparation for your Promise. Let the waters of His Spirit overtake you and carry your towards your destiny! Become drenched in the presence of the Lord!

Chapter Tips

#11: God will go out of His way to meet us in our desolate places.

When God needs to get a Word to His people, He will move Heaven and Earth to make it happen. Samaria was not in the "GPS," but Jesus received an assignment to go to the Well. No matter where you are at in your life, God is not far away. The Word says, "Where can I go from Your Spirit? Or where can I flee from Your presence? **8** If I ascend into heaven, You *are* there; If I make my bed in hell, behold, You are there. **9** If I take the wings of the morning, And dwell in the uttermost parts of the sea, **10** Even there Your hand shall lead me, And Your right hand shall hold me." (Psalm 139:7-10)

#12: The waters of His Spirit are able to provide life to dry and dead places.

There is hope! The woman of Samaria sought relief in the dry recesses of companionship. She assumed her heart's void would be mended through the temporary love of men, but did not realize it was a mere band aid on a gaping wound that could only be restored by the Well of Living Water, Jesus Christ. Her "date with destiny" at the well provided the life-sustaining water of the Spirit needed to quench and dry and desolate place in her life. Will you

The Wilderness

dig deeper today? Don't just settle for what is on the surface, burrow into the dimensions of your heart, and unearth the well of Living Water in your life!

#13: Seek to "know" the Father, not just know "of" Him.

The word "know" in the Bible has several meanings, but one most important meaning comes from the Hebrew word *yada*, which means to know, have intimate knowledge of something or someone. This word is used all throughout scripture in reference to marriage, intimately joining together with one flesh, or making love. "Now Adam *knew* Eve his wife, and she conceived and bore Cain..." (Genesis 4:1a) The woman of Samaria had only heard of the Messiah, but He came that she might intimately know Him, or have knowledge through relationship, that He was her Lord. She no longer needed physical intimacy to patch up her wounds; the Lover of her Soul had found her! Seek to know God intimately and you will never thirst again!

"*Most blessed among women is
Ja'el. The wife of He'ber the Kenite;
"Blessed is she among women in
tents.*"

Judges 5:24

Chapter 5

Promoted in the Spirit

"The Wilderness of Tekoa"
(The Place of Maturity)

"Then Jesus was led up by the Spirit into the wilderness to be tempted by the devil." (Matthew 4:1)

Promotion is a time of great celebration. Our accomplishments are rewarded with elevation and public affirmation. This can be one of the greatest moments in our lives, a time of recognition that affirms our identity and reveals our faithfulness and dedication to others. Immediately after God proclaimed, "This is My beloved Son, in whom I am well pleased," He was led into His wilderness. Be prepared to go through your process after a promotion in the Spirit. We would expect Jesus to go straight into ministry after being lifted up by His Father. It seems evident for one to go to the next level as soon as they are elevated, right? Not so in the Kingdom. In the Kingdom of God, it is just the opposite. We must first go down before we go up. The Word tells us that Jesus first descended to the lower parts of the earth before He ascended to Heaven. The Word also admonishes us to humble ourselves.

The Wilderness

"Therefore humble yourselves under the mighty hand of God, that He may exalt you in due time," (1 Peter 5:6)

Jesus could have taken this moment as the "green light" to go into His earthly ministry, but if He had, He would not have been prepared to deal with the tests, trials, temptations and tribulation awaiting Him. Too many of us think we are ready for the calling of God on our lives. We cut every corner possible to obtain a title or position, so God can use us. Let me promise you that God is not in your mess. Stop asking God to put a stamp of approval on "your" ministry, "your" gift, or "your" calling. If you refuse to walk through your wilderness, you are not ready for the Kingdom! Find somewhere to serve and allow God to purge you of yourself, so you are prepared for the greater levels of responsibility and maturity. This is not about you. You are not only hurting yourself, but ultimately, if you force your way into something prematurely, you will hurt many other people as well.

Jesus is the Son of God, if He had to go through His process of maturity, what makes us think we are exempt for ours? Are we so prideful and arrogant to think we can withstand the attacks of the enemy without first having been tried in our wilderness? This is absurd! Our wilderness is a training ground. It is designed to purge us of our selfish desires and motives and to replace it with humility, brokenness, and ultimately maturity in Christ. It is a place where we are tested to our limit, in order to reveal if we are prepared for what God has for us, or if we will break and compromise our faith for what the enemy will offer us. Many of us miss the mark several times during our wilderness experience. We see several instances in the Word, from Abraham to Elijah, where those who went before us failed their tests. But we also see that God did not give up on them. Instead, He continued to pursue them and push them towards their purpose. The Children of Israel failed many tests along their journey through the wilderness, and many did not enter the Promised Land, but those who submitted to the process, eventually entered into the land God had prepared for them.

In today's society, no one wants to endure the process to receive their promotion. People want it now, and if they cannot get it the right way, they will compromise and push their way into positions God did not intend for them, which not only harms them, but many others. The problem with this is that we are, by nature, selfish people. Our motives, or intentions, are usually self-indulged attempts to gain the praise and approval of man; to feel as if we have achieved some sort status in our lives. As Believers in Christ, our goal is not the praise of men, but the approval of God.

"For do I now persuade men, or God? Or do I seek to please men? For if I still pleased men, I would not be a bondservant of Christ." (Galatians 1:10)

We have to be very careful of steering clear of the ways of this world and not following after the ways of God. If you seek the approval of man, you will get temporary satisfaction, but end up with eternal consequences. Make a choice to walk through your wilderness, so God can transform your life and lead you into your purpose. We cannot expect the blessing and favor of God, but refuse the work of Christ in our lives. God does not work this way. God expects us to grow and to be transformed by His Word and by His Spirit. Let Him have His way in your life.

The Wilderness

"They rose early in the morning and went out to the wilderness of Tekoa; and when they went out, Jehoshaphat stood and said, 'Listen to me, O Judah and inhabitants of Jerusalem, put your trust in the Lord your God and you will be established. Put your trust in His prophets and succeed.'" 2 Chronicles 20:20

The Wilderness of Tekoa means the place of setting up tents, fastening down, or the place of maturity. It is a place where we make a determined decision to follow the Lord and to put our full trust in Him. We become established in His Word and His ways. No longer do we follow our own ways, but we submit ourselves not only to God, but to those He has placed over our lives to spiritually lead and guide us towards our purpose. It is very crucial to have a covering over your life. Our gifts and calling should be subject to someone of spiritual maturity and authority. In doing so, we eliminate our natural desires and tendencies to rebel and step out prematurely. In surrendering our lives and submitting ourselves under the leadership of someone else, we allow God access to move freely in and through us.

Ja'el was a very insignificant Biblical character, according to worldly standards. She is only mentioned in one chapter, but her heroism will forever be recorded in the annals of history. Not much is mentioned about her past or her lineage, but we can pull so much from just a few short scriptures about this bold woman of God. The Wilderness of Tekoa is known as the place of pitching tents, or the place of "maturity". Ja'el lived in a place called Zaanannim, which means "moving". She not only was a housewife who knew how to take care of her family, but she was also very skilled in "pitching tents". The constant moving from place gave her the experience needed to face

Deborah G. Hunter

what would be her ultimate test of faith, and her mark in Biblical history.

The character of Ja'el is also boldly noted in these short passages of scripture. Ja'el is first mentioned in the Bible as the "wife of Heber the Kenite". She was a submitted woman. She had a covering, and must have brought honor and esteem to her household to be mentioned as his wife. It says that she went out of her tent to meet Sisera, the commander of the army of King Jabin, a king who had oppressed the children of Israel for about twenty years. A prophetess and judge at this time in Israel was Deborah, also first mentioned in scripture as "the wife of Lapidoth". One very important thing to note here is that a woman in ministry must be submitted to her husband, or submitted under a covering. God does not release rebels into ministry, nor does He allow you to skip the process of your wilderness to be elevated. Maturity and accountability are vital keys to walking in the purpose of God for your life. This foundation is clearly displayed in these two short statements in the lives of both Deborah and Ja'el. God needed us to see that He had called them both, and they were qualified through their submission to their earthly headship.

Let's dig a little further into the character of Ja'el. In Judges Chapter four, verse eighteen, it says:

"And Ja'el went out to meet Sisera, and said to him, "Turn aside, my lord, turn aside to me; do not fear." And when he had turned aside with her into the tent, she covered him with a blanket. 19 Then he said to her, "Please give me a little water to drink, for I am thirsty." So she opened a jug of milk, gave him a drink, and covered him." (Judges 4:18-19)

The Wilderness

My God! What a woman of integrity, honor, and maturity! She called him lord. Ja'el was a woman who understood authority. He may have been an oppressor, but this did not affect the character of this mighty woman of God. As mature believers in Christ, we will see a lot that we don't agree with, and many times, we want to lash out at those in authority that we expect to do the right things. We know they are held to a higher standard and should be upholding this position with the greatest of character. Our job is not to judge them, but to honor them, respect them and yes, COVER them, just as Ja'el did. This is a sign of spiritual maturity. We are called to walk out the Word of God, period. Our feelings and emotions should not have precedence over the Word in our lives. Because she submitted to her husband, submitted to God, and honored this man in authority, God was able to use Ja'el to fulfill her destiny. It pays to be submitted.

Another aspect of Ja'el's maturity is seen in her offering her "best" when it was not even asked of her. Sisera requested water, but Ja'el offered him milk. How often do we offer up that which is our least, when God always requires our best fruit, or offering? We saw in Genesis the tragedy that occurred because Cain refused to offer the Lord his firstfruit. We think we can hide our selfish intentions from God, but He sees and knows all. He is Omnipresent, everywhere at all times, and sees every motive and intention, whether good or not so good. This act was also seen as divine strategy in that water was the "appropriate" thing to offer someone coming into her tent from battle, but she chose the milk instead. The milk allowed Sisera to relax and fall asleep, giving her the opportunity to slay him in his sleep. She was full of character and wisdom. Ja'el could have skipped saying lord and gave this evil man a piece of her mind. She didn't even have to give him a drink of water, but it was not in her character to turn someone away from the service of her life. She had the heart of a servant. Don't expect God to use you to change this world if you are not willing to change yourself! This is not about us, but solely about bringing about His plan and purposes in the earth, and that takes a great deal of submission and maturity.

I can't help but imagine how the impact of Deborah, the prophetess and judge over Israel, also had upon Ja'el. So many women were oppressed during these times and were only seen as housewives, mothers, and keepers of their homes. To have a prophetess and a judge over Israel that was a woman had to have had a tremendous impact upon the women living during this time. Deborah was also a woman of great character and right standing with God. She not only possessed a great prophetic gift, but God anointed her with the authority to release it over a nation.

"And she would sit under the palm tree of Deborah between Ramah and Bethel in the mountains of Ephraim. And the children of Israel came up to her for judgment." (Judges 4:5)

Deborah means "bee," or the Word. We get the name "spelling bee" from the derivation of her name. She had the Word of God in her mouth for the nation of Israel. She, too, was prepared in the conduit of her wilderness before she was released into the ministry of the prophetic, as well as the office of judge. Deborah had to first submit to her head before she could faithfully and effectively judge a nation. The process is absolutely pertinent for each of us, no matter if we are called as a housewife or a prophet to the nations. Deborah's submission and obedience led her into her Promised Land, her purpose for which she was created. The scripture above says she would sit under the palm

The Wilderness

tree of Deborah. Palm trees in the Bible represent a place of righteousness. It is a place where we can go for shade, shelter, and wisdom. It reveals much about the life of Deborah, as well as reveals how God relates to His Church, the Bride. Through her lifestyle and relationship with the Lord, Deborah was able to stand in the place of authority for so many others.

"The righteous shall flourish like a palm tree, He shall grow like a cedar in Lebanon. 13 Those who are planted in the house of the Lord shall flourish in the courts of our God. 14 They shall still bear fruit in old age; They shall be fresh and flourishing, 15 To declare that the Lord is upright; He is my rock, and there is no unrighteousness in Him." (Psalm 92:12-15)

This reveals the life of Deborah. She planted herself in the will of God and flourished and grew in maturity and right standing with the Lord to the point where others were able to receive refreshing underneath of her "palm tree," or leadership. Her deep relationship with God began to spill out of her personal life into the realms of her community and nation. Your life should be an example to someone else. Your time in your wilderness is not to kill you or to destroy you, but to transform you and lead you into the perfect will of God for your life. In Christ, we are to lay down our lives, our will, in order to be a light and an example to someone else. Just as the children of Israel crossed over the Red Sea out of the bondage of Egypt, we too experience great excitement when we become saved. All of our senses become magnified in the light of God's love for us, and we are propelled into the Word of God and into the service of the Lord. We want to immediately be used of God, and elevated into our gifts and calling, but what we don't understand is that just because we are saved does not mean we have

Deborah G. Hunter

been transformed. We need to go through our "process," our wilderness.

As I stated earlier, I catapulted in my walk with God. I developed the heart of a servant very early on and purposed to serve God and people with my whole heart. I had so much joy during this time and found great fulfillment in my life. I had no desire to be seen, and titles were the furthest thing from my mind. I served faithfully in the Children's Ministry in every church I attended, and began to fall in love with the ministry of dance, which thrust me into even greater intimacy with God. I even asked God not to put me in any leadership position, because I did not need a title to serve God or His people. But in my ignorance and naivety, I did not understand that God had a purpose and a calling greater than my mind was willing to take me. He did, indeed, elevate me without one inclination of it occurring. I battled with it greatly to the point of wanting to tell my pastor I did not want to be in this position. We were called into a leadership meeting, assuming we were just going to be a support element in a new city our pastor was seeking to plant a church. When I opened up the agenda, I looked down and saw my name with this title in front of it. My heart sank and from this moment on, I fought with God, asking Him to let me just be Deborah. This is the truth! This began my journey into my wilderness. Some will fight against the calling, while others pursue it to such an extent that the position is more important to them serving God. No matter the situation, we ALL are destined to enter our process of preparation.

Notice how I said earlier in the Kingdom, elevation does not automatically lead you into the next level, but leads you into your wilderness. We have to be trained to hear the voice of God, and to

The Wilderness

operate in order, so that we will minister His heart and not our own. Our will has to be totally surrendered to the Lord, in order to be used as Deborah was. It does not state specifically her wilderness experience, but through the words of the writer of Judges, it is most evident that she endured her process and God found her faithful to elevate her as a prophetess and judge of Israel. Stay in your process!

The scripture also states that Deborah sat in between Ramah and Bethel in the mountains of Ephraim. Ramah means a place of height, usually seen as a place of pride, self-seeking or idolatry. It was known as a place of arguing, back biting, confusion and turmoil. In contrast, Bethel means "the house of God," or the presence of God. Why would she sit in between such disparity? God called her as a judge, and as children of God, we must understand that we, too, are called to judge the nations of this world. We are not called to pass judgment, but we are called to judge between righteousness and unrighteousness. In our early stages of salvation, we are not equipped or experienced enough in the things of God to judge rightly. All too often, we end up on the side of judgment, as opposed to spiritually judging a situation. We end up hurting people and offending them, instead of allowing the Spirit of God to penetrate their lives through our submission, obedience, and yes, maturity in spiritual things.

I wish I could say that I passed my tests in these areas, but unfortunately, I did not in some. I was beginning to hear from the Lord, and He would reveal things to me in dreams, as well as in my prayer time. Because I knew the Word of God intimately, I assumed I was supposed to release it. And in one instance, I didn't release a Word God specifically told me to share with someone. I was afraid I would offend or hurt this person. I wasn't mature enough to under-

Deborah G. Hunter

stand that God had already prepared their heart, and it was the time to share it. When I did finally reveal this Word, it was the wrong time, in the wrong place, and with the wrong spirit. Instead of building this person up, I tore them down. We have to understand that God does everything in His timing and in order. If we step outside of this divine order, just because he "spoke" it, does not mean He will use you now to release it! Our process is extremely crucial.

Deborah's example proved not only to refresh the children of Israel in their times of chaos and confusion, but it extended into the life this woman named Ja'el. Through the life of this prophetess and judge, this mighty woman of God, Ja'el was able to discern her appointment with destiny and to operate in divine order with character, honor, integrity, and grace.

Be sure that you submit your gifts and calling under the authority of a submitted, obedient, and tested mentor, or spiritual leader. Their life should be an open book, not one of perfection, as this is not attainable by any man, but one that is laced with failures and triumphs. Every leader should have experienced their own wilderness, in order to help lead someone else out of theirs.

Both Deborah and Ja'el are great examples of spiritual maturity. These women of God were submitted, obedient, and possessed the utmost character of Christ in their assignments. They were used by God because of their willingness to grow in Him and learn of Him. They laid down their lives, so that others could live out their purposes through them. These precious women will forever live on in the lives of God's people throughout the generations. What will be your legacy? Let the life of Deborah and Ja'el influence you to live for Christ and

The Wilderness

die to self. Your purpose is attached to nations of people. Allow them to see your relationship with God, and imitate your walk with Him.

"but imitate those who through faith and patience inherit the promises." (Hebrews 6:12b)

Chapter Tips

#14: Elevation in God's Kingdom is going down before you go up!

So often, we are tempted to skip the process of our wilderness in order to step out and do what "God" called us to do. Worldly promotion always seeks its own, and never journeys down the road of self-denial. The Kingdom of God is not fashioned in this manner. The Kingdom motto is "To go up, you must go down." Promotion from God requires total surrender, sacrifice, and submission. It is no longer your will, but His will. The Word said He had to first descend to the lowest parts of the earth before He could ascend to the throne of His Father. Let go of selfish ambitions and pick up your cross.

#15: God does not use rebels; He releases faithful, humble, submitted, and obedient people.

Selfishness, pride, greed, arrogance, and egotism are plaguing our world today. Everyone wants to be in the spotlight and to hear their names mentioned across the airwaves. This is not only among the unsaved, but has slowly crept into the chambers of our congregations. If we are not recognized or elevated quick enough, we take matters into our own hands and either elevate ourselves, or run somewhere to get someone to agree with our mess and lift us up. REBELLION! The Word says, "Humble yourselves in the sight of the Lord, and He will lift you up."

The Wilderness

(James 4:10) I know when He lifts, He will cause everything to fall in place. Be patient and trust Him.

#16: Submit yourself under tested leadership.

The Bible warns us that in the last days, many false prophets and teachers will arise and spew out false doctrines and teachings. These people will deceive and manipulate, but there are those who have not compromised their faith or beliefs for wealth, status, or fame. God has placed shepherds in your life to cover you and to speak His Word over you. Be sure that they have a lineage of wisdom, experience, and integrity. If they are always agreeing with you and letting you do what you want, you may want to do a "background" check.

#17: God will use the most "insignificant" people to carry out His divine plans.

Moses was a stutterer, Jacob was a liar, David was an adulterer, Miriam was a gossiper, Jeremiah was depressed and suicidal, Paul was a murderer, and so was Abraham, Noah was a drunk, Hosea's wife was a prostitute, Elijah was burnt out, Mary was lazy, Peter didn't know how to shut up, Zechariah was short, and all of us have our own shortcomings and weaknesses. God has proven all throughout scripture that He does miraculous things through the hands of everyday people like you and me. Ja'el, though not mentioned in the Word until this particular portion of scripture, was groomed by the Lord for this moment in time. Her elevation was in His hands and in His timing. Wait on the Lord, but serve while waiting.

"Now a certain man found him,
and there he was, wandering in the
field. And the man asked him,
saying, "What are you seeking?"

Genesis 37:15

Chapter 6

From the Mountaintop to the Valley

"The Wilderness of Paran"
(The Place of Wandering)

"Now after six days Jesus took Peter, James, and John his brother, led them up on a high mountain by themselves; and He was transfigured before them. His face shone like the sun, and His clothes became as white as the light. And behold, Moses and Elijah appeared to them, talking with Him." (Matthew 17:1-3)

The desire to rule in high places is the oldest travesty in history. From the betrayal of Lucifer, to the disobedience of Adam and Eve, man has been tempted to seek power and authority, instead of learning and growing in their place. We love the mountaintop experiences with all that comes with it. We are mesmerized with the influence and status that is afforded us in these places. There is lack for nothing, and the worries of the world seem all but untraceable in this

The Wilderness

realm. The problem with this mindset, very similar to that of promotion, is that mountaintop experiences are just that, experiences. They are not continual, and will eventually lead into a valley. Promotion in the Kingdom, after great testing in the wilderness, releases us into our calling, but mountaintop experiences are more of a reward designed to show us the blessing of God. He will allow us to walk in favor, but we must understand that adversity will happen to us all. We are not exempt from the trials of life just because we are Christians.

Valley experiences will come in many forms and for many different reasons. God allows us to enter into valleys to bring us back to reality, to reveal to us that material things and status are not what sustains us, but relationship with Him. He takes these times to humble us and to bring balance back into our lives after we have strayed away due to the exposure of the high places. He doesn't want things to overtake us, but rather wants us to utilize the blessing of God to bless other and to build His Kingdom. Other ways we enter into valleys is through attacks of the enemy, attacks from others, and just our own disobedience which leads us there. No matter the instrument, God always makes a way of escape.

Though the mountaintops provide great peace and joy for us, the valley affords us greater opportunities to learn and grow. It is in times of great adversity that the human spirit is able to rise above its natural surroundings and soar to heights unimaginable. In the valley, we come to realize that the possibilities in God far outweigh any blessing He could ever supply. This is a revelation of a difference. What is more important to you, what God can give you or what you can learn from Him that will allow you to walk in true power and authority in this earth? I don't know about you, but the answer is

Deborah G. Hunter

obvious to me. I want more of Him! I know with Him, I am covered, protected, and provided for. No matter what I will face, He will be there with me.

"Yea, though I walk through the valley of the shadow of death, I will fear no evil; For You are with me; Your rod and Your staff, they comfort me." (Psalm 23:4)

> Your valley is not your destination, but a passageway to your next mountaintop.

Valleys are considered "low" places, whereas wildernesses represent "dry" places. Going from the mountaintop to the valley can be very devastating emotionally and mentally. It is a very drastic change and can cause us to blame God if we are not grounded in the Word of God. But when we understand that He has purpose in every season, we are more likely to grow and learn *through* the valley, just as the Psalmist David did in the scripture above. Your valley is not your destination, but a passageway to your next mountaintop. The quicker you learn the lessons needed in your valley, the sooner you will be able to experience the blessing of God.

We know the children of Israel spent forty years wandering in the wilderness. From one dry place to the next, they murmured and complained and wished they were back in Egypt. They didn't understand that they were now free; free to find themselves in the God who saved them. Instead, they were willing to go back into slavery, because it was familiar to them. It was easier to know what they were to expect, instead of journeying with the Lord to find their reason for existence. To them, their mountaintop was Egypt. How many of us compromise our Promised Land because we are more comfortable on

93

The Wilderness

our "mountaintops"? We know there is more out there, but fear of losing what we have paralyzes us and causes us to forfeit our true destinies. This is surely a trick of the enemy. He uses fame, fortune, and the "spotlight" to lure us into these high places, attempting to make us believe God is blessing us or giving us His favor. If He tried it with Jesus, why do you think he will not try it with us?

"Again, the devil took Him up on an exceedingly high mountain, and showed Him all the kingdoms of the world and their glory. 9 And he said to Him, "All these things I will give You if You will fall down and worship me." (Matthew 4:8-9)

We see this spirit so rampant in our world today. Everyone is seeking fame and fortune, and desires their name in lights. Competition in every area of the marketplace has shifted to some of its greatest heights, and it is considered a "dog eats dog" kind of world. There is no more respect, no more loyalty, and no more compassion towards our fellow man. It is so evil that people are killing one another, in order to the "top" at their game, or craft. The spirit of deception is so strong in our world today that people in "high places" literally control every aspect of our society. If you don't sell enough music or bring in the numbers to the box offices, they will remove you from those "mountaintop" highs and leave you so broken and depressed that you have no hope of even living anymore. This spirit is very real, and has found its way into the Body of Christ. Nothing is sacred anymore. We don't understand that the Kingdom of God does not operate as the world does. Our chief goal is not fortune or fame, it is the Kingdom. "But seek first the Kingdom of God and His righteousness and all these things will be added to you." (Matthew 6:33) The enemy has crept into our sacred assemblies and tainted the gifts of Believers. We

94

Deborah G. Hunter

have even invited him in through our ignorance. Over the last decade or so, the Church has adopted this idea that we need to bring the "marketplace" to the house of God. It has caused the spirit of pride, greed, and "status" to infiltrate what was meant to be holy. If we would just pick up the Word of God and read it from time to time, we would not fall into as many traps as we do today.

"Then Jesus went into the temple of God and drove out all those who bought and sold in the temple, and overturned the tables of the money changers and the seats of those who sold doves. [13] And He said to them, "It is written, 'My house shall be called a house of prayer,' but you have made it a 'den of thieves.'" (Matthew 21:12-13)

> The enemy will always amplify that it is all about you, that no one understands what you are going through.

Jesus Himself understood the implications of the "high places," or the mountaintops. Satan offered Him all the kingdoms of the world if He would just bow down and worship him. This is what many Believers find themselves caught up in today. Instead of seeking the Kingdom, they allow that little voice that sounds LOUD to persuade them that their gifts are not being recognized in the Church. Important to note: out of the two voices you will hear, the enemy's is small and LOUD, while the voice of the Lord is noted as being the "still small voice". The enemy will always amplify that it is all about you, that no one understands what you are going through. He will tell you to "go for it" without any seeking or praying about it. His desire is for you to be lifted up in pride and self-seeking agendas to the point where you dismiss God altogether in your

The Wilderness

life. Do not be deceived! Understand that in this walk with God, we will surely go through valleys and wildernesses, so that we are trained to walk as He walked and not lose ourselves in the "high places."

God allows valley experiences to teach us great lessons in life. Suffering does not always feel good, but it absolutely produces much fruit in our lives. It leads us to place of total surrender to the Lord and provides for us a level of trust that is unmatched. It is in difficult times where we learn to rely upon God, not in our times of blessing and increase. In our valley's, we are better able to see God for who He is; our Protector, our Provider, our Healer, our Redeemer. If we don't go through our valley, how will we ever know who God is? If we stayed on our "mountaintops," we would never have need of the Father. Sadly, we see this happening in Christendom. We preach about the Christ, but have no relationship with Him. His name is used to preach fabulous sermons that have people running to the altar with money, it is used in songs that are void of His Spirit, all in an effort to make money, and it is manipulated in movies to draw unsuspecting crowds that refuse to see that HE is nowhere in it! The name of Jesus is very profitable, and the enemy will use every tool available at his disposal to manipulate it for his means, including you and I. Don't be deceived! Embrace your valley, so God can build up His Spirit within you.

The Wilderness of Paran is considered the "Place of Wanderings". From our study of the children of Israel, we know that their journey was only supposed to be an eleven day passage. If they had submitted and surrendered to the Lord, they would have learned valuable lessons designed to propel them into their Promised Land. Instead, they did everything but thank God for rescuing them from the strong arm of Pharaoh. Their brief trip turned into a forty year span that left the wilderness as the burial ground for many of them. It took them only three days to travel from the Wilderness of Sinai to the Wilderness of Paran. Some lessons, if learned quickly, will lead you out of wilderness, or valley, but if you buck up against the work of God in your life, you may find yourself spending the rest of your life wandering in search of your Promised Land.

"Now it came to pass on the twentieth day of the second month, in the second year, that the cloud was taken up from above the tabernacle of the Testimony. 12 And the children of Israel set out from the Wilderness of Sinai on their journeys; then the cloud settled down in the Wilderness of Paran... 33 So they departed from the mountain of the Lord on a journey of three days; and the ark of the covenant went before them for the three days' journey, to search out a resting place for them." (Numbers 10:11-12, 33)

Their next lesson, however, would prove fatal for many, as they spent the next thirty-eight years in the Wilderness of Paran. They wandered, some, for the rest of their lives. Don't allow pride and rebellion to keep you from entering your destiny. It is a sad thing to see people wander their entire lives when all they had to do was submit to God's will and His process for their lives. One of the best ways to endure these wilderness, or valley, times is to incorporate a lifestyle fasting and prayer. We must focus our attention on the Lord, instead of the situations around us. In Matthew Chapter four, after Jesus was led up by the Spirit into the wilderness, it says he fasted for forty days and forty nights. He was being prepared for the temptations the enemy was about to unleash upon Him. When God sends us into a wilderness, there is great purpose for it. The trying of our faith produces patience, and every test passed creates in us the spirit of an over-

The Wilderness

comer. We are then "prepared" for those mountaintops, because we will understand how to appreciate the blessing without it overtaking our lives and taking us away from God.

Though valleys and wildernesses are necessary, God does supply us with mountaintop experiences. All throughout the Gospels, we see where God would lead Jesus up to the mountaintops to pray. These are times of great refreshing and spiritual growth. We become intimately enthroned by the love, compassion, and grace of the Father. Our faith is restored and our trust in Him is deepened greatly. But we know that Jesus eventually had to come down from those mountains. His time in the presence of His Father strengthened Him and built Him up to face all that was down in the valley. Let's take a look at a destined mountaintop experience prepared by God for the disciples Peter, James, and John.

> If we stayed on our "mountaintops," we would never have need of the Father.

"Now after six days Jesus took Peter, James, and John his brother, led them up on a high mountain by themselves; [2] and He was transfigured before them. His face shone like the sun, and His clothes became as white as the light. [3] And behold, Moses and Elijah appeared to them, talking with Him. [4] Then Peter answered and said to Jesus, "Lord, it is good for us to be here; if You wish, let us make here three tabernacles: one for You, one for Moses, and one for Elijah."

[5] While he was still speaking, behold, a bright cloud overshadowed them; and suddenly a voice came out of the cloud, saying, "This is My beloved Son, in whom I am well pleased. Hear Him!" [6] And when the

Deborah G. Hunter

disciples heard it, they fell on their faces and were greatly afraid. (Matthew 17:1-6)

The disciples were very aware that Jesus frequently spent time on the mountaintops. They knew these times produced great fruit in the ministry of Jesus, as each time He came down, He had life-changing words or it propelled Him into great seasons of healing and deliverance. Peter, James, and John must have been elated to be invited up the mountaintop by Jesus. Would they get to experience the same level of presence that their Lord encountered on this mountain? Little did any of them know that this mountaintop experience would change their lives forever? It impacted Peter to such an extent that he wanted to pitch tents for Jesus, Moses, and Elijah and stay there as long as they could. What Peter failed to realize was that he was in the midst of preparation. God was revealing to him and the other disciples that Jesus was exactly who He said He was, and God confirmed it, not only through the transfiguration, but with the witness of Moses and Elijah. Peter did not have the death of Jesus on his mind, even though a few verses earlier, Jesus was preparing him for just that. Peter was focused on the mountaintop, while Jesus was being prepared for the valley. We have to keep our hearts and minds focused on the King-dom. We lose sight of the Kingdom when temporary mountaintop experiences grab our attention, and we think we have reached our apex.

If it was up to Peter, Jesus would have stayed in His glory on the mountaintop, instead of walking through the Valley of Kidron on His way to Calvary. Jesus had to rebuke Peter several times for not understanding the importance of His journey. He wanted the moun-taintop experience with Jesus, but was not willing to walk through the

The Wilderness

valley with Him. We have to learn how to walk through the valley with others, before we expect to partake in their mountaintop experiences. Character is developed in the valley and in the wilderness. God is not interested in what makes us happy or comfortable; He is concerned with our spiritual development. Your time and test in the valley is completely up to God. He knows exactly what we need and how long we need to stay there. Our willingness to accept the work in our lives will determine if our stay will be extended, as was the children of Israel in the wilderness.

> Peter was focused on the mountaintop, while Jesus was being prepared for the valley.

God prepared me early on in my walk with Him. He instilled the importance of humility, character, and integrity. My heart was washed with His Word, inspired by His Spirit, and before I knew it, He has placed His heart in mine. I understood that "high places" were very dangerous if I did not have His wisdom concerning them. God quickly taught me to steer clear of worldly appetites and the need to hold a title. I was the same with or without a nametag, and the only One I was lifting up was Jesus. He also admonished never to lift a man or woman of God up as a celebrity. My prayer is that the Body of Christ would turn from the current state it is in with this "celebrity status" that is ravaging our churches. This is not God's will for us, and it absolutely grieves His heart. There are times and seasons where the need to elevate us will come, but it is ONLY for His ultimate purposes, not our own. Guard your heart and stay close in His presence. He will lead you.

Deborah G. Hunter

Throughout it all, we will have valley lows and mountaintop highs. It is crucial to understand the importance of each, so we are not entangled with the world or depressed in the valley. Trust God with all of your heart and allow Him to teach and train you in His perfect will. As you allow Him to lead you, you will grow in wisdom, knowledge, and understanding.

Chapter Tips

#18: Mountaintop highs will eventually lead to valley lows.

Everyone, at some point in their lives, will experience a mountaintop high and a valley low. It is inevitable. Ask some of the most famous people on earth and many of them will tell you they wish they could just live "normal" lives. The fast life drains and depletes us of crucial valley experiences needed to develop character, as well as balance in our lives. We see, too often, celebrities or political figures who live their entire lives on the "mountain-top," and lose themselves there, because there has been no development in the valley. Don't lose yourself in the spotlight. Put the focus on Him, and make His name great and He will lead you.

#19: Be mindful of "high places".

"For we wrestle not against flesh and blood, but against principalities, against powers, against the rulers of the darkness of this world, against spiritual wickedness in *high places*." (Ephesians 6:12) Media creates Hollywood and the "beautiful life" to look so appealing. Mansions, limos, sports cars, clothes, jewelry, awards, accolades, notoriety, status, fame, and the like are encouraged and applauded, as it is the "American Dream!" What we don't realize is the higher you go, the greater the demons. Satan and his angels reside in the "heavenlies," or the area of the atmosphere between Heaven and Earth. He cannot offer you Heaven, as it is not his to give; he was kicked out. But what he can try to do is offer us the "highest places" on Earth, so we can bow down and worship him. You can't bow down to what is beneath you, you can only offer obeisance to what you are looking up to. Look to the Lord your God and put that devil under your feet!

#20: Stay focused on what God has called you to do.

So many distractions are sent to knock us off our course and cause us to forfeit the call of God upon our lives. Many things will be masqueraded to look like the will of God, but if you are faithful to your process in the wilderness, you will be prepared to spot the real from the fake. Know who you are and what God has called you to do and you will not be deceived.

#21: Resist the urges of temptation.

"Submit yourselves therefore to God. Resist the devil, and he will flee from you." Period! (James 4:7)

"For I am convinced that neither death nor life, neither angels nor demons, neither the present nor the future, nor any powers, neither height nor depth, nor anything else in all creation, will be able to separate us from the love of God that is in Christ Jesus our Lord."

Romans 8:38, 39 (NIV)

Chapter 7

Be Ye Separate

"The Wilderness of Shur"
(The Place of Isolation)

Therefore "Come out from among them And be separate, says the
Lord. Do not touch what is unclean, And I will receive you."
(2 Corinthians 6:17)

The life of a Nazarite in Biblical times was a very honorable lifestyle. Nazarenes were considered a people set apart by God. There
were very strict guidelines they were to follow in order to be used by
God. From before conception in the womb, God spoke to the wife of
Manaoh, from the city of Zorah, that she would conceive a son. The
Lord admonished her to be careful not to drink wine or any other
similar strong drink and not to eat anything unclean while she carried
her son in the womb. Immediately after the proclamation of opening
her womb, the angel of the Lord began to lay out, one by one, specific
instructions to the woman concerning the child to be born.

"For behold, you shall conceive and bear a son. And no razor shall
come upon his head, for the child shall be a Nazarite to God from the

The Wilderness

womb; and he shall begin to deliver Israel out of the hand of the Philistines." (Judges 13:5)

Living the Nazarite vow was a public acknowledgement of cutting off anything that would hinder one from pleasing God and walking in the fullness of their calling from birth. We will study several of the restrictions of the Nazarene lifestyle and how it pertains to us, as Believers in Christ Jesus, today. The first guideline given to the mother, while the child was in womb, was to refrain from wine and strong drink. The purpose of this was to keep oneself from worldly pleasures. The wine was made from fermented grapes, so it was seen as rotten, which would lead us into the sin of the world. Abstaining from strong drink was a fast of sorts, designed to draw them closer to the Lord. For us, this means we are called to live in this world, but not of it. God wants us to keep ourselves unspotted from the world. The lusts of this world like money, fame, and status draw us away from God. He desires intimacy with us, so we have to understand that we cannot have both. Guard yourself from these things and replace them with the Word of God, prayer, fasting and just time in His presence, whatever that means for you.

Another instruction was to grow your hair long, and never to cut it. This symbolized a person was living under the authority and covering of someone else. Today, we are covered and under the authority of Jesus Christ. As we submit our lives to Him, we reveal to the world a greater testimony than that of the early ritual of the Nazarenes. When we live our lives according to the Word of God, we reveal our total surrender to the Lord and others will be impacted by our obedience. Make the choice to be a light in someone else's life.

Finally, the Nazarite was not to go near a dead body. If they did, they would be considered unclean, or spotted by spiritual death. As Christians, we are commanded to steer clear of any and all sin. When we don't, it is very easy to fall into worldly things, and our spiritual integrity is tainted. So many people are falling away from Christ today. The world is sucking the life out of them, and leaving them helpless and hopeless. We are compromising our spiritual walk by accepting worldly practices and ideas, all in the name of not offending those who don't know Jesus as their Lord and Savior. Our salt is losing its flavor and our light is growing dim, because we are allowing what is "unclean" into our daily lives. It is very important to guard the gateways of our lives, our eyes, ears and mouths. What we allow in will eventually come out. The Nazarenes understood this principle and guarded their lives to the utmost, so God could reveal His glory through them. Their acts of obedience were a foreshadow of what was to come through the life, burial, and resurrection of Jesus Christ, and how we, as Christians today, would submit our lives under His covering. What beauty in a surrendered, submitted, and yes, separated life!

> Our salt is losing its flavor and our light is growing dim, because we are allowing what is "unclean" into our daily lives.

Jesus was Himself considered to be of the Nazarene lineage. The Word of God in the Old Testament prophesies that Jesus would settle in Nazareth.

The Wilderness

"And he came and dwelt in a city called Nazareth: that it might be fulfilled which was spoken by the prophets, He shall be called a Nazarene." (Matthew 2:23)

What better example for us to follow than Jesus Christ! He separated Himself unto God and His will for His life. Multiple times throughout the New Testament, we see our Lord separating Himself from the crowds to go to the mountaintop to pray. He fasted often and kept Himself unspotted from the world. Though He was tempted, just as we are, He was free of sin, the ultimate Nazarene.

At this juncture in my wilderness, I did not understand why the Lord was removing people from my life? I was always a relational person. Relationships were, and still are, very important to me, but what I did not realize was certain friendships/relationships were toxic. God revealed to me that I was serving as a god in their lives. No matter what spiritual counsel or advice I gave, they had no intention of seeking God on transformation. They wanted someone to agree with them, instead of surrendering and allowing God to show them their reflection in the mirror. I loved so deeply that I didn't want to see people go through the wilderness, but I did not understand that this is EXACTLY where God needed them to journey through. He also began removing people from my life who were not supposed to be in it anyway.

Please seek the Lord for the friendships, relationships, and even business partners that HE has preordained for you. The people you are connected to bear a huge role in your destiny. Be sure that the right people are in your life at the right time. This by no means implies a haughty or egotistical stance in regards to people. We are called to love, pray, and bless even our enemies, but what it does urge is to be very selective in who you allow into your intimate space, and who you spend most of your time with. God spoke a very clear word to "guard my heart" during this time. I did not receive it for myself, because I was so caught up in trying to help others. I assumed it was for someone else, until He really began to open this word up to me. He was trying to protect me from what was about to occur.

The last instance I want to touch upon when it comes to God separating us from others is very similar to the tradition of the Nazarenes. They were separated in such ways, so God was able to use them. Sometimes, He will separate us from people that we would never expect to be separated from. None of the aforementioned situations apply, and you are absolutely caught off guard when God removes someone from your life who has done nothing wrong, who was loyal, who supported you, and who you thought would be in your life forever. We have to trust God that He knows what and who we need in our lives, and in what season. Seasons change, and we have to move with them. If we bring people into new seasons that were ordained for our last season, we will hinder what God wants to do in our lives. This is not easy, and takes a lot of maturity. One way to look at it is if God is taking you into a new season, He is doing the same for them. He has purpose for every one of His children. We allow offense to take root when we are not grounded in His Word and led by His Spirit.

I have witnessed the spirit of pride and arrogance overtake people who are being shifted into a new season. They make people feel as if something is wrong with them, and that God is removing them from their life because they have such a tremendous calling upon their lives. God does NOT work like this! This is a classic reason why some

The Wilderness

people are led into their wilderness, because there are some things that need to be removed from their lives before God can use them. If Spirit does not line up with Word, it is NOT God! It is that simple.

I fought against God in several instances. I did not separate myself when I knew deep down that He was removing people from my life. I held on as long as I could, and it not only affected my life, but their lives as well. True spiritual maturity hears God, trusts God, and does exactly what He tells us to do, no matter what our feelings say. God is not concerned with our emotions; He is focused on our growth and getting us to our expected end. Don't fight God. Listen to Him, trust Him, and do what He tells you to do. He loves us, and has mapped out our journeys. He will lead us every step of the way...all of us. We are all a piece to the ultimate puzzle of life. Pray that your brother and sister will, too, reach their expected end. The wilderness is all about developing in the image and likeness of our Father. At the end of the day, we should be doing what He has already done.

> If Spirit does not line up with Word, it is NOT God! It is that simple.

The Wilderness of Shur is considered the "Place of Isolation", or separation. Shur was the first place the Israelites stopped after exiting the Red Sea. The representation is very crucial, as the children of Israel had been in slavery all of their lives. They knew nothing else but bondage and oppression. God had to stop them in this place of "separation" not only to show them they were not who Pharaoh said they were, but also to reveal to them that they no longer had to think this

112

Deborah G. Hunter

way of themselves. When we come to Christ, our minds have to be transformed by the Word of God, how He sees us. (Romans 12:2) Crossing over from the Red Sea was their "salvation" experience. Now, God needed to isolate them to pour into them who He was and who they were in Him.

"So Moses brought Israel from the Red Sea; then they went out into the Wilderness of Shur. And they went three days in the wilderness and found no water. [23] Now when they came to Marah, they could not drink the waters of Marah, for they were bitter. Therefore the name of it was called Marah. [24] And the people complained against Moses, saying, "What shall we drink?" [25] So he cried out to the Lord, and the Lord showed him a tree. When he cast it into the waters, the waters were made sweet. There He made a statute and an ordinance for them, and there He tested them, [26] and said, "If you diligently heed the voice of the Lord your God and do what is right in His sight, give ear to His commandments and keep all His statutes, I will put none of the diseases on you which I have brought on the Egyptians. For I *am* the Lord who heals you." (Exodus 15:22-26)

The Israelites were immediately separated into their first wilderness journey. They had to learn very quickly that though they were out of slavery, they still had to learn obedience. Except, this obedience was not beaten into them. God gave them free will to choose to follow Him. They had to understand that their new freedom did not give them a pass to do whatever they wanted, but He was producing character through their process. They encountered the city of Marah, and the waters were bitter, they were not able to drink from these springs. Please understand that your journey through your wilderness will produce bitter seasons, but be encouraged, God will provide relief as you cry out to Him. When Moses cried out to God, He provided a "tree" to place in the waters to make them sweet. This tree represents the cross of Jesus Christ. As you allow the Lord to enter into your situations, the bitterness will flee and the sweet fruit of the Spirit will appear.

Be patient and keep your heart and your ears open to His Spirit. Embrace your wilderness and allow Him to transform you. Though God holds the depths and lengths of our wildernesses in His hands, we can prolong our time there through disobedience and rebellion. Don't be as the children of Israel were wandering in the wilderness for forty years. God has too much for us to do in this earth. Too many people need us whole and complete, and in our rightful authority.

One Nazarine in particular, Sampson, was set apart from his mother's womb. We discussed earlier the angel of the Lord meeting his mother and giving her specific instructions how to carry him and raise him. She followed the directions and trusted God, to the point of persuading her husband, Manoah, that God would not have revealed Himself to them, accepted the offerings, and spoke of their future son if He was going to kill them. She was absolutely convinced that God would carry out His promise in their lives.

"So the woman bore a son and called his name Samson; and the child grew, and the Lord blessed him. 25 And the Spirit of the Lord began to move upon him at Mahaneh Dan between Zorah and Eshtaol." (Judges 13:24-25)

The Nazirite vow of separation from the "unclean" things allowed the Spirit of the Lord to rest upon those who faithfully observed these rituals. It says he grew and the Lord blessed him, and the Spirit of the Lord moved on him. Many of us want God to use us. We desire the opulence without the obedience. We want the anointing without the agreement. But I promise you, if you do not set yourself apart from the things of this world, God's hand is not upon you. There are way too many self-professed apostles, prophets, evangelists, pastors, teachers and every kind of leader out there in the Body of Christ who are operating in witchcraft! They have refused the process of the wilderness, because they felt they were ready for ministry. They could not wait for God to do His work in them, so they took it upon

> We desire the opulence without the obedience. We want the anointing without the agreement.

themselves to start their own ministries. Many are deep in sinful lifestyles, but still walk boldly into that pulpit every Sunday morning thinking God is using them, and that His Spirit is upon them. This is rebellion!

"For rebellion is as the sin of witchcraft, And stubbornness is as iniquity and idolatry. Because you have rejected the word of the Lord, He also has rejected you from being king." (1 Samuel 15:23)

His Word is Truth! He does not lie. Surrender, submit, and repent! He will forgive you and begin His perfect work in you, once again. This does not mean you will ever walk in this position of authority again, it means He can and will restore you to your rightful place in fellowship with Him. I have seen, time and time again, ministers of the Gospel fall into sin and temptation and EXPECT to be restored to their positions. This is pride and arrogance! It is selfishness! Your only desire should be asking the Lord to forgive you, as well as those you have hurt, and allowing God to heal you, deliver you, and set you free. This word in I Samuel says He "rejected" him from being king. God cancelled the assignment on this king's life to rule and reign in this kingdom. He may have pulled him down from authority, but God's desire is to restore us all. Restoration does not mean re-instating, and does not mean restoration in the sense of worldly titles or positions, but the posture position of our hearts and right standing with Him. Saul, in this scripture, had many times to repent and turn from his evil and rebellious ways, but his position meant more to him than his character. His pride, arrogance, and jealousy caused him to not only lose his kingdom, but also his life. Let us all examine our motives and intentions daily, so that we can walk freely in God's will for our lives.

Samson was raised in great separation. He knew the call of God upon his life, and was trained in the ways of the Lord. He understood the implications of the "unclean," but the temptations of his wilderness were inevitable. Just as Jesus was led into His wilderness, so, too, was Samson. After every promotion, there is a season of testing. Would he pass his test? The Word says he went down to Timnah. The scriptures jump from him being born, growing, being blessed by God, and the Spirit of the Lord being upon him in one verse to the next verse in Chapter 14 of him leaving from underneath of his covering to venture "down" to Timnah. Each of us will be sent out into our wilderness to test if we are ready for our assignments. He saw a woman who was the daughter of the Philistines and wanted her. He told his mother and father of her, and boldly told them to "get her for me as a wife". Now Samson had not known this woman nor had he ever laid eyes on her

Deborah G. Hunter

before this moment, but he had been separated all of his life in the ways of the Nazirites. He knew the Lord and was trained in the Spirit.

"But his father and mother did not know that it was of the Lord- that He was seeking an occasion to move against the Philistines. For at that time the Philistines had dominion over Israel." (Judges 14:4)

Many of us don't understand why God does what He does at times. We assume that God will plan out our lives to our "liking," or that He will line it up with our own wills. We see all throughout scripture, otherwise. We must understand that we are here on this earth on assignment. It is for His purposes, and when we give our lives to Him, it is no longer about us and what we desire, but wholly what He wants to do through us to reach a lost and dying world. Ask yourself if you are truly ready to lay down your life for Christ.

On his way to meet this woman, the Spirit of the Lord came strongly upon Samson. He had traveled with his mother and father, according to the Word, to the vineyards of Timnah. One of the instructions of the angel of the Lord for the Nazarite was not to drink wine or any strong drink for that matter. A young lion met him on his journey, and the Bible tells us that he tore it apart with his bare hands. God was showing him something through this test. It was a warning, reminding him of his vows as a Nazarite. He was dangerously close to compromising himself. He defeated the lion and nowhere does it mention he ate or drank of the vine, he passed this test. On our journey through our wilderness, on our way towards our Promise, temptations will present themselves to knock us off track. We must remind ourselves of the purpose and stay focused. But we also need to know that "Greater is He that is in us, than he that is in the world." (1 John 4:4)

The Wilderness

Charles Spurgeon said it this way:

"If that roaring lion, that goes about continually seeking whom he may devour, finds us alone among the vineyards of the Philistines, where is our hope? Not in our heels, he is swifter than we: not in our weapons, we are naturally unarmed: not in our hands, which are weak and languishing; but in the Spirit of God, by whom we can do all things. If God fight in us, who can resist us? There is a stronger lion in us than that against us."

Now when he had returned to Timnah to retrieve his wife, he was met along the way by the carcass of the lion he has slain. Let's stop here for a moment. This was his second test. Nowhere did it say Samson fell in love with this woman, or that he had feelings for her. It simply states in several verses that he saw her and that she pleased him. Many times, God will give us an assignment to fulfill. We know the plan and we understand the requirements to carry it out, but what we "see" becomes more enticing to us that what we know about the assignment. Samson cared more about what it looked like to him, rather than how it looked to God. His pleasures kept leading him to do things against what he knew to be right.

"After some time, when he returned to get her, he turned aside to see the carcass of the lion. And behold, a swarm of bees and honey were in the carcass of the lion. 9 He took some of it in his hands and went along, eating. When he came to his father and mother, he gave some to them, and they also ate. But he did not tell them that he had taken the honey out of the carcass of the lion." (Judges 14:8-9)

Deborah G. Hunter

The anomaly in this is one, Samson knew he was not to touch anything dead, or it would make him unclean. And secondly, God had just used him to defeat this animal. Why would he then go back and eat of something God used him to destroy? God had not spoken to him that this animal would be sustenance for him. By allowing his senses to take over, instead of the wisdom he was raised with, Samson allowed his pleasures to override purpose. He not only ate of the honey himself, but he gave to his parents, unbeknownst to them, of an unclean animal. The further we allow our pleasures to entice us, the greater sin will grow in our lives, and it will not only affect us, but those around us. Be very mindful to keep your eyes on Jesus. Your focus should always be on the Lord and what He is calling you to do. The enemy will try to tempt us in every way he can to keep us from fulfilling our purpose. Separate yourself!

The Levitical priesthood was commissioned along the exact same lines as Nazarites. In fact, the Nazarenes were considered of the "lineage" of the Levitical priests. In each generation, God

> In each generation, God wants a people who will set themselves apart for Him.

wants a people who will set themselves apart for Him. It wasn't until Jesus of Nazareth came that obedience flooded the realms of the Spirit and our High Priest ushered in the age of grace. He was the embodiment and fulfillment not only of the Levitical priesthood, but also of Nazarite lineage. He fulfilled every vow, every law, all the while ushering in the grace of God. "He did not come to do away with the law, but came to fulfill it." (Matthew 5:17)

The Wilderness

Samson continued to sink deeper and deeper into sin. His pleasures turned into pride, and he began to allow the circumstances around him to distract him from his purpose. The woman he desired betrayed him, and she was given to one of his companions. He came back and wanted to marry her, but his father informed him that she was given away. Each time something did not go his way, he went on a rampage. Though he was veering off the pathway of righteousness, God was still with him. It says the "Spirit of the Lord" came upon him mightily each time he went up against something or someone. The lesson in this is someone can be greatly anointed and empowered by the Holy Spirit, but spiritually immature. They use the power of God to manipulate situations for their own benefit. This was the road Sampson was traveling down, very fast.

He used people and situations for his own pleasure and completely neglected his purpose for going into this area. He was going deeper into his wilderness experience, and blaming everyone else for his disobedience. He finally fell in love with a woman in the Valley of Sorek named Delilah. He trusted her to the point that he told her all of his heart, he revealed the secret of his strength.

"Then she lulled him to sleep on her knees, and called for a man and had him shave off the seven locks on his head. Then she began to torment him, and his strength left him." (Judges 16:19)

The longer we stay in sin, in due time, the enemy will catch up with us. His "love" of women put him on a path of destruction. He will use deception and manipulation to lure us into his web, so he can kill, steal, and destroy everything that concerns us. The story of Samson is a foreshadow of Jesus' temptation in the wilderness. Three separate times, satan came to tempt Jesus, but each time, He spoke the Word only and the enemy had to flee. What if Samson had done the same? He surely knew the consequences of each sin: the wine, the dead carcass, and the cutting of his hair, yet he neglected each one in pursuit of his own desires. Both of these instances with Jesus and Samson were consequences of 1 John 2:16; one chose the Father, while the other chose the world.

"For all that is in the world, the lust of the flesh, and the lust of the eyes, and the pride of life, is not of the Father, but is of the world."

In today's spiritual circles, the temptation of what is "available" is flooding the minds of our leaders, as well as lay members. By seeking "marketplace" strategies to grow our churches and bring in more members, we have been deceived by the ways of the world. We "see" what looks good, just like Samson, but God is not in it. We use our spiritual authority to excuse our sin away, and manipulate and blame others for the mess we get ourselves into. We have to separate ourselves from the world, and trust God to do the drawing. When we operate outside of the set order of God, we cannot expect Him to be with us. He will lift His hand from upon us.

"And she said, "The Philistines are upon you Samson!" So he awoke from his sleep, and said, "I will go out as before, at other times, and shake myself free!" But he did not know that the Lord had departed from him."

My heart aches each time I read this passage of scripture. An anointed man of God, predestined with purpose, filled with the Holy Spirit, set apart for great works, and his life was filled with great

The Wilderness

tragedy. This was not God's plan for Samson's life. He had an assignment and he was led in the right direction, his footsteps were ordered, but he still had to make the choice to follow the leading of God and continue to separate himself, not follow his own desires. We all do this from time to time, and we have all suffered the consequences in one way or another. God desires more for His children. He is seeking obedience, not sacrifice. We don't have to wait until the very end of our lives to serve Him in Spirit and in Truth. We can choose now to obey His Word and be led by His Spirit. I have read the story of Samson many times throughout my life, but it was not until the writing of this book that my eyes were opened to a very small portion of scripture.

"Then Samson called to the Lord, saying, "O Lord God, *remember me, I pray*! Strengthen me, I pray, *just this once*, O God, that I may with one blow take vengeance on the Philistines *for my two eyes*!" [29] And Samson took hold of the two middle pillars which supported the temple, and he braced himself against them, one on his right and the other on his left. [30] Then Samson said, *"Let me die with the Philistines!"* And he pushed with all his might, and the temple fell on the lords and all the people who were in it. So the dead that he killed at his death were more than he had killed in his life. [31] And his brothers and all his father's household came down and took him, and brought him up and buried him between Zorah and Eshtaol in the tomb of his father Manoah. He had judged Israel twenty years. (Judges 16:28-31)

Samson cried out for God to "remember me, I pray" (the lust of the flesh). Throughout the entire assignment, God was reaching out to Samson. He sent warning after warning to him, but he refused to heed His voice, but now, he wanted God to remember him. He also said,

Deborah G. Hunter

"Strengthen me "just this once". He was operating in the previous situations with the mindset that he did not have to ask God for anything (the pride of life). He assumed that the Spirit of the Lord would always be with him, no matter what.

Don't allow yourself to be deceived by the enemy. Don't wait until tomorrow, or the next time, to obey God. Obey Him now! "Do not harden your hearts as in the rebellion, in the day of trial in the wilderness," (Hebrews 3:8) Samson's heart hardened to the Spirit of God. He no longer followed the ways of God, but his own path. The next thing that struck me when reading this scripture was that he said, "That I may with one blow take vengeance on the Philistines "for my two eyes" (the lust of the eyes). Samson was FINALLY taking responsibility for his disobedience. He, without physical sight, was now finally "seeing" with the eyes of his heart.

He was finally in a place of total surrender to the Lord, and he wanted to make it right with God. He wanted to finish what God had started in his life. His last words to God were, *Let me die with the Philistines!*" The Bible says that in his last final battle, Samson killed more in his death than he did while living. His high calling was fulfilled, and he was now separated fully unto the Lord. As I said earlier, don't wait until the end of your life to obey and follow God. Separate yourself now, and let God use you to bring many others to Him. We can be in this world, but not of this world if we stay grounded in His Word and led by His Spirit.

"For such a High Priest was fitting for us, who is holy, harmless, undefiled, separate from sinners, and has become higher than the heavens;" (Hebrews 7:26) He alone is our great example!

Chapter Tips

#22: There is a time in our lives where we all will be required to separate from the world.

We are all shaped by our pasts, and each experience lends growth and maturity, no matter how messed up it may have been. We learn from our mistakes and gain wisdom through them. But there is a time in our lives where are told to "put away childish" things, so we can move to greater heights emotionally, mentally, spiritually, and physically. Some people cannot move into their future, because they are comfortable in their past. God is saying to separate from anything that will take you back. Let go and move forward!

#23: Don't try to keep people in your life that God is trying to remove.

God predestined your life according to His perfect will. He knows where you would be born to who would serve as the incubator for your passageway into this world. He knows the time of our entrance and the time of our exit. Our Father puts kings in power and removes them, all according to His divine providence. How much more does He divinely place people in our lives, and removes them when their season is over. Don't fight to keep those in your life He is trying to take out. Because He knows each sea-

The Wilderness

son you will journey through, He also knows who is assigned to go with you. Be pliable with Holy Spirit. He will speak to you and lead you.

#24: Obedience is better than sacrifice.

Please just listen and obey! Some say experience is the best teacher, but clearly there are some things God says to just do, so you won't have to go through pain, disappointment, and heartache.

#25: Don't wait until the end of your life to obey God!

We think we have all the time in the world to submit and surrender to the Lord. We don't want to let go of the things or people that make us happy in this world. A perfect statement, "I'll come to God when I am ready, but I am going to have fun as long as I can." Don't get caught up with those who disobey and be consumed with them. God told Lot to separate, to leave. If he had not obeyed, he would have been destroyed along with Sodom and Gomorrah. "Be separate!"

"Do not be anxious about anything, but in everything, by prayer and petition, with thanksgiving, present your requests to God. And the peace of God, which transcends all understanding, will guard your hearts and your minds in Christ Jesus."

Ephesians 4:6, 7

Chapter 8

No Where to Turn

"The Wilderness of Edom"
(The Place of Compromise)

"Nevertheless I have this against you, that you have left your first love." 2 Kings 3:8

Solomon was considered the wisest man to ever live. His wisdom far exceeded his years, and God was pleased with him. Ironically, he was also considered one of the greatest fools to ever walk the earth. How can someone be considered in both of these categories? Why would someone with such great wisdom, who knew God intimately, walked with the Lord, and heard the voice of His Spirit clearly, fall into compromise? Just as we learned from Samson, God called him, prepared him, and sent him out. It is up to us to take what God has given us, and walk faithfully in our purpose.

After the death of his father, David, Solomon was instated as king over Israel. He was very young, most likely in his teens, and he was completely sold out to God and the plans and purposes of the Lord.

The Wilderness

His complete obedience and faithfulness unlocked doors for this young man in the Spirit.

"Now, O Lord my God, You have made Your servant king instead of my father David, but I am a little child; I do not know how to go out or come in. ⁸ And Your servant is in the midst of Your people whom You have chosen, a great people, too numerous to be numbered or counted. ⁹ Therefore give to Your servant an understanding heart to judge Your people, that I may discern between good and evil. For who is able to judge this great people of Yours?"

¹⁰ The speech pleased the Lord, that Solomon had asked this thing. ¹¹ Then God said to him: "Because you have asked this thing, and have not asked long life for yourself, nor have asked riches for yourself, nor have asked the life of your enemies, but have asked for yourself understanding to discern justice, ¹² behold, I have done according to your words; see, I have given you a wise and understanding heart, so that there has not been anyone like you before you, nor shall any like you arise after you. ¹³ And I have also given you what you have not asked: both riches and honor, so that there shall not be anyone like you among the kings all your days." (1 Kings 3:7-13)

Solomon's beginning was pure and honorable. His heart was authentic, and God perceived this and it touched the Lord. He not only gave him wisdom and understanding, but He gave him that which he did not ask for, riches and honor. When God is pleased with our lives, He not only blesses His people, but He reveals His glory in and through us. What endearment! Solomon touched the heart of God.

Deborah G. Hunter

As Solomon grew in wisdom and grace with God, His kingdom expanded. The Lord did exactly what He promised over Solomon's life, but his rapid success caused him to seek wealth, fame, and notoriety, instead of the God who honored him with it. He still worshipped God, but he compromised the Truth through his lustful desires. We have to guard our hearts and guard our minds as Believers. The enemy knows our weaknesses and will surely test us with them. He perverts the blessing of God and twists our thoughts concerning the purpose of His blessing. When Truth begins to be compromised, we know that we are being deceived somewhere. Be very mindful of seeking the applause of men, rather than the approval of God. Solomon gathered a harem of over one thousand women, seven-hundred wives, princesses, and three-hundred concubines from all walks of life. He developed strong ties with leaders from other nations, and people knew the name of King Solomon, as if he was God. His heart turned away from the Giver, and his wealth and fame consumed him.

> Be very mindful of seeking the applause of men, rather than the approval of God.

We see this rapidly infecting the people of God today. The enemy is tainting every aspect of Christian society, so it can lose its affect on the world. He doesn't care if we go to church. In fact, he comes and sits with us, at times, because one, we welcome him in, and two, because God is nowhere in the midst of compromise, chaos, and confusion. Our lusts have turned into full-blown sin and we have forgotten who the Lord is and what He has done for us. We want the blessing, but reject the One who blessed us. We want His benefits

The Wilderness

without the responsibility of integrity and character. We honestly think God is anointing us and using us, elevating and increasing us. God does not promote sin. He does not sponsor disobedience. The moment we compromise the Word of God, we quench His Spirit from our lives, and His hand is lifted from us. Solomon's father, David, knew all too well the consequences of this.

"Do not cast me away from Your presence, And do not take Your Holy Spirit from me." (Psalm 51:11)

How often is God nowhere in our church services today? He is silent in our fellowships, because we have not invited Him in. We manipulate services to convince people that God was there and moved mightily when He was not even in the midst of our mess. Our lustful desire for our name to be in lights and for people to shout at our "revelations" opens our minds to the torment of the enemy. He will use deception to persuade us that God is using us and the spirit of pride and arrogance creep in and manifests itself in absolutely ungodly ways. We start to make excuses for our sins, our disobedience, and seek others who will agree with us. God help us! Compromise is like cancer. It spreads very quickly if not cut off at its root. It is a downward spiral that leads to great immorality.

I told God when He commissioned me to start my publishing company that I would operate in character, honesty, and integrity, and that I would purpose to give Him glory for it all. The first five years in operation, my company flourished in ways unimaginable. The favor He bestowed upon it was mind-blowing. I determined to read every manuscript myself and if I did not sense His hand upon it, or if I discovered anything that was not of Him, I would not accept it for

Deborah G. Hunter

publication. Mind you, I turned down quite a few manuscripts over the years, and some of them were from professed pastors who penned all kinds of foolishness. I knew God was not in it, and it would not bring glory to His name. One particular book that came our way, stumped me. As I read the story, it was definitely amazing what I read on paper. The miracles and deliverance was astounding, and I asked the Lord, "Is this You?" My spirit was a little unsettled. The author was kind and gentle, and proceeded to speak very highly of my business and my family. I prayed and asked God to bring books to us magnifying His healing and deliverance in people's lives. I had the desire to publish true life stories impacted by the power of God. This was the first book that came in after I made this request to God, so I immediately thought this was answer to prayer.

I had an abrupt change in the business as book sales fell and people were not publishing books. After five prosperous years, I went into a dry place. I was desperately praying for "rain" to come into the business, and sure enough, a door opened up. My spirit began to become even more unsettled during the process of publishing this book. This author began to prophesy to me almost daily through emails, and at first, they were right on point, so I assumed this was God. After a while, it started to get a little weird. I was now at the point of asking God to forgive me for not heeding the promptings of His Spirit. Crazy things began happening in the business. We lost five computers to systems crashes and several back up hard drives with multiple contracts and manuscripts stored on them.

Delays and confusion were happening that never occurred before in five years of business, and all hell was breaking loose in this company. As I sat very still one day at my desk, I repented and asked

The Wilderness

God to close this door that I had opened. Not only did I compromise the integrity of my promise to God, but now, I was in direct disobedience to Him. God revealed to me the witchcraft released through this book, and that it was not of Him. I cancelled the publication of this book, but the strange things were still occurring. I prayed and asked Holy Spirit to show me what I was missing, and sure enough, I heard the Lord say, "Delete EVERY file of the book off of your computers, hard drives and emails." WOW! It was just as clear as that! I did exactly that, but still no end to the confusion. As I sat crying and praying that God would intervene, I heard that "still small voice" say, "There is a copy still here." Okay, now many people have not experienced witchcraft like this, and some may not believe it, but let me tell you, this was very real. My family experienced this first hand, as well as some of our staff. Another dear friend and staff member had very similar occurrences take place at her home. She, too, had a copy of this manuscript in her possession. I told her what was occurring in my office, and what God had revealed to me, and she disposed of the copy in her possession. The confusion ended in her home.

I ripped through file cabinets, boxes, desks, book shelves, drawers, and everywhere I could possibly look for this manuscript, and it was nowhere to be found. I was angry, because I remember reading this manuscript clearly. It was one of very few that we received printed out and mailed. I recollect a note attached to it and a printed out photo of the author, and I didn't throw away any of the ones I received in the mail, so it had to be somewhere! Again, frustrated and at the end of my rope, I heard the voice again say, "Pull out the drawers of the file cabinets." I did just as the Spirit of God said, and it was stuck behind one of the drawers. I have to be honest, I have witnessed witchcraft before and seen it in operation several times, but this was personal. I

Deborah G. Hunter

was very angry, and began to anoint and pray over my business, the computers and everything that concerned my business, but I had to face the reality that this was my fault. I had compromised the Truth, what I felt in my spirit, for the "rain" over my business, but what I brought was a curse. Thankfully, in disposing of this manuscript, everything returned to normal. Our systems were fine, the confusion ceased, and great light was shone on this situation. God closed the door for me. I cannot thank Him enough for blessing me in spite of my disobedience.

Solomon, just like Samson, did not heed their warnings either, but they just outright rejected God's promptings and slid so far into disobedience, compromise, and rebellion that they succumb to it. Don't allow yourself to surrender to the sin that is trying to overtake you. Make a choice to live by the Word of God and to be led by His Spirit, so that your purpose and destiny is not aborted. Live for Him and learn of Him. Study and meditate on His ways and be transformed by them. These anointed men of God did not live out their full potential. God still worked all things together for His good; He will complete His plans, but how sad not only for them, but for their generations to come. Because they refused to walk through their own wilderness, they were not able to walk into their Promised Land. And God cut off their blessing as well.

Esau was another example of compromise in the Bible. He and his brother Jacob were twins. They fought one another coming out of their mother's womb. While Esau was the first to come out, his brother Jacob grabbed onto his heel, thus adopting the name "heel-catcher". All throughout their childhood, Esau was considered his father's favorite. He was a mighty hunter and would always bring back game

The Wilderness

from hunting and cook for his father. Esau, being the eldest, had priority in birthright. He was to be the predecessor of his father's estate. Esau was aging and his time in the field began to weary him. One day, when coming in from hunting, Jacob, his younger brother, was fixing a pot of stew.

"Now Jacob cooked a stew; and Esau came in from the field, and he was weary. [30] And Esau said to Jacob, "Please feed me with that same red stew, for I am weary." Therefore his name was called Edom. [31] But Jacob said, "Sell me your birthright as of this day." [32] And Esau said, "Look, I am about to die; so what is this birthright to me?" [33] Then Jacob said, "Swear to me as of this day." So he swore to him, and sold his birthright to Jacob. [34] And Jacob gave Esau bread and stew of lentils; then he ate and drank, arose, and went his way. Thus Esau despised his birthright." (Genesis 25:29-34)

> Don't ever allow yourself to get to a point in your life, business, or ministry where you get so tired that you compromise your "birthright".

Esau was tired. He had spent his entire life hunting in the fields, and lost all hope of anything better for his life. He was completely exhausted, so he sold his birthright to his brother Jacob. Don't ever allow yourself to get to a point in your life, business, or ministry where you get so tired that you compromise your "birthright". God has great plans for us all, and long life and prosperity, in every area of our lives, is His desire.

136

Deborah G. Hunter

"And let us not be weary in well doing: for in due season we shall reap, if we faint not." (Galatians 6:9)

Life is not easy, and even in Christ, we all are destined to walk through some very difficult times. We get tired because we don't see the manifestation of God's promises coming to pass in the time we expect them to. We become worn out doing what we feel He has called us to do, but there is no visible reward in it. Exhaustion sets in, and eventually, we come to a crossroad of compromise. Maybe it is better if I just give up on this company that God told me to start. What if I just stop writing and go get a nine to five job? I will be better off if I just let this dream go, and try something else? I am tired of not being recognized; somebody out there will appreciate me? I am faithful and loyal, but they don't see it, so I may as well leave? Have you found yourself asking these questions before, or even now? Weariness is very real, and if we don't put it in the hands of God, we will find ourselves compromising the very promise of God our lives.

Right now, there is a heavy spirit of weariness over the Church. Times are becoming more evil by the day, and we have reduced the house of the Lord to, as Jesus coined it, "a den of thieves". With the global Church shifting, we have seen within the last two decades an emergence of celebrity-style preachers. I am sure most did not have the intentions of ending up in this melting pot, but when you seek man's advice, counsel, and ways, you will surely end up compromising the integrity of God's Church. It is becoming an "event-oriented" structure, and church boards are sitting down daily trying to come up with marketing strategies to bring in people and money. Pastor's faces are being plastered across book covers and billboards, YouTube and Television talk shows.

The Wilderness

We have missed it! The spirit of compromise entered in and we have all but kicked the Lord out of our weekly services. Satan could care less if we meet every Wednesday, Sunday, Easter, Palm Sunday, Mother's Day or Christmas. In fact, he will come and fellowship with us if we reduce, or water-down, the Gospel of Jesus Christ. This is real people of God. We are in an age of great deception. We are finding ourselves "sleeping with the enemy" all in an effort to "build the church". I can promise you that we are not building the church, but erecting our own empires. This is a tough pill to swallow, but nevertheless, it is Truth. This world wants nothing to do with our God. But the Word of God prophesies a time when the wealth of the wicked will be laid up for the just. This will be a time of great prosperity, not just financially, but in every realm. We cannot reduce the promises of God to merely money. Wealth encompasses a vast expanse of blessing; peace, joy, love, faith, kindness, and every fruit of the Spirit. The problem is, through weariness, we have focused our attention on money and fame, a quick fix to our issues. We think money will solve the problem that only our "wilderness" is able to answer. You cannot get peace from money. The spotlight is not going to provide joy in your life. In fact, if we do not allow the process of preparation to unfold in our lives, we will lose ourselves in those very lights. The Word of God tells us what to seek after.

"But seek first the Kingdom of God and His righteousness and all these things will be added to you." (Matthew 6:38)

Don't sell your "birthright" to the highest bidder or in Esau's case, the lowest. This world is not concerned about your Jesus, but trust that they will try anything possible to profit off of the name! From books, music, movies to every area of the marketplace, we have allowed the

Deborah G. Hunter

world to infiltrate what God has commanded us to separate. Just as we saw with Samson, we are making what is holy, unclean. We are bringing the world into our holy places and allowing every kind of spirit to be released into our churches and into the lives of God's people. This MUST end! When we compromise this way, God removes His hand, His anointing, from every area of our lives. He is no longer with us. Just as Samson, it is devastating to get up one day and realize that God has lifted His hand from our lives.

Break these curses today and repent. Turn to God and ask Him to close all of the doors you allowed open. Be patient and allow Him to do His perfect work in your life, so He is able to trust you with the true riches of Christ. After all that God put in Solomon's hands, in the end, was taken from him.

"So the Lord became angry with Solomon, because his heart had turned from the Lord God of Israel, who had appeared to him twice, [10] and had commanded him concerning this thing, that he should not go after other gods; but he did not keep what the Lord had commanded. [11] Therefore the Lord said to Solomon, "Because you have done this, and have not kept My covenant and My statutes, which I have commanded you, I will surely tear the kingdom away from you and give it to your servant. [12] Nevertheless I will not do it in your days, for the sake of your father David; I will tear it out of the hand of your son. [13] However I will not tear away the whole kingdom; I will give one tribe to your son for the sake of My servant David, and for the sake of Jerusalem which I have chosen." (1 Kings 11:9-13)

Trust God to take you through your process. His reward is greater than anything this world can offer you.

The Wilderness

Trust God in your process, so that He can lead you into your Promised Land. When God's hand of blessing is upon you, there is peace. "The blessing of the Lord makes one rich, And He adds *no sorrow* with it." (Proverbs 10:22, emphasis mine)

Chapter Tips

#26: When God releases the Blessing over your life, there is great responsibility attached to it.

Jacob was considered cunning, a manipulator and a liar. From the moment we are introduced to him in the Word, we see him grabbing the heel of his brother Esau, trying to surpass him to get out of the womb. That did not happen, so the younger brother led his entire life planning how he would eventually scheme to be the greatest. Be very mindful of trying to surpass what God has for YOU. The grace He has given another for their assignment may not be the amount you need to carry it out. Count the costs before you try to step into another man's anointing.

#27: Your true "birthright" is too valuable to sell.

Being born into a royal family is a big deal, especially for a boy. His entire life, he is groomed to become king and take over his father's throne. He is trained and disciplined to walk upright and will do everything he can to ensure nothing hinders him from walking in his full potential and calling as the next king. So it is with Believers today. We are being prepared to walk in the fullness of who God created us to be, and nothing is worth losing our eternal inheritance.

The Wilderness

#28: The world will make you compromise something. Trust the Lord, and go through the process.

"All that glitters is not gold," a common saying that we have all heard, right? Well let's take it a little further. "All that glitters is not GOD." The enemy loves to twist and manipulate everything good in God, so that we will sell ourselves short of the Promise. Walk in truth and wisdom, and trust the Lord in your process. To know something is of God, just test it according to the Word of God. If it leads you to compromise in any way, it is not Him.

#29: His ways are higher than our ways.

We may not always know what God is doing in the midst of our tests and trials, but one thing we do know, He is in control of it all! He sees the beginning from the end, and has mapped it all out to work together for our good. Don't try to outthink God. You will lose every time! Put your faith in Him, and let Him lead you.

"The sacrifices of God are a broken spirit, A broken and a contrite heart— These, O God, You will not despise."

1 Peter 4:10

Chapter 9

The Beauty of Brokenness

"The Wilderness of Beersheba"
(The Place of Surrender)

"Reproach has broken my heart, And I am full of heaviness; I looked for someone to take pity, but there was none; And for comforters, but I found none." (Psalm 69:20)

Society teaches us to live life to the fullest and that we deserve to be happy, so do so by any means necessary. We are fashioned to live according to our flesh, so when introduced to Christ, we find it hard to living according to the Spirit. The ultimate goal in the life of the Believer is transformation, but transformation cannot occur without brokenness. Our will is not tampered with by God, so it is completely up to us if we want God to come into our lives and change us.

The Wilderness

This is probably the single most difficult process, or wilderness, in the life of a Believer. No one likes to be broken, it doesn't feel good, and we are trained to reject anything in our lives that takes us out of our comfort zone.

Job was a man of upright character. He was a man who followed the Lord and upheld his faith and integrity. Job taught his children in the ways of the Lord, and God blessed him beyond measure.

"There was a man in the land of Uz, whose name was Job; and that man was blameless and upright, and one who feared God and shunned evil. [2] And seven sons and three daughters were born to him. [3] Also, his possessions were seven thousand sheep, three thousand camels, five hundred yoke of oxen, five hundred female donkeys, and a very large household, so that this man was the greatest of all the people of the East. [4] And his sons would go and feast in their houses, each on his appointed day, and would send and invite their three sisters to eat and drink with them. [5] So it was, when the days of feasting had run their course, that Job would send and sanctify them, and he would rise early in the morning and offer burnt offerings according to the number of them all. For Job said, "It may be that my sons have sinned and cursed God in their hearts." Thus Job did regularly." (Job 1:1-5)

Job's life was impeccable, almost perfect. His ways were right before God, and he even presented burnt offerings on behalf of his children, to cover them if they had fallen away from the Lord. What a man! It is obvious that he exuded the true essence of prosperity that we spoke of earlier. Every area of his life was overflowing with sheer blessing. What more could Job want or need in his life? God's plans, as we found out earlier, far exceed the depths our minds are able to imagine. He knows each of us by name, and maps out each of our journeys by hand.

"Now there was a day when the sons of God came to present themselves before the Lord, and Satan also came among them. [7] And the Lord said to Satan, "From where do you come?" So Satan answered the Lord and said, "From going to and fro on the earth, and from walking back and forth on it." [8] Then the Lord said to Satan, "Have you considered My servant Job, that there is none like him on the earth, a blameless and upright man, one who fears God and shuns evil?" [9] So Satan answered the Lord and said, "Does Job fear God for nothing? [10] Have You not made a hedge around him, around his household, and around all that he has on every side? You have blessed the work of his hands, and his possessions have increased in the land. [11] But now, stretch out Your hand and touch all that he has, and he will surely curse You to Your face!" [12] And the Lord said to Satan, "Behold, all that he has is in your power; only do not lay a hand on his person." So Satan went out from the presence of the Lord." (Job 1:6-12)

There are times when we absolutely understand why we are going through tests. Our disobedience sets forth in motion the winds of correction, chastisement, and even at times, rebuke we need in order to get back to the place of right standing with God. We understand these "wildernesses," and even though it is painful, we know how and why we are there. But what do you do when your life is committed to living for God, upholding character and integrity, and leaving a legacy of Christ for your family, and God decides to take you through a wilderness? God was bragging on His son Job. Satan was out walking up and

The Wilderness

down the earth seeking whom he could devour. His sights were not even on Job, because he assumed God's hand of protection was upon everything concerning him. God approached satan with this opportunity to test Job, because He knew what was inside of him.

Our walk in Christ is a continual process of growth. Nowhere does it tell us that we will reach perfection here on this earth. God sees us at each interval of our life and knows the intents of our hearts and what it will take to get us to the next level. Job was well off in every sense of the word, but what happens when we hit the ceiling of our faith? What travesty to be in a place where there is no more need, or desire, to go higher or believe God for more? Again, we are not talking about material wealth, thought that may come, but of greater intimacy and revelation of who the Father is and what His plans are for our lives. To know that He constantly thinks of you and I, from the day we are born to the day we pass away from this life. Every second of every minute of every day, He is shifting and maneuvering our lives in orchestra with His will. Job was about to enter into the most significant wilderness experience of his life.

> What travesty to be in a place where there is no more need, or desire, to go higher or believe God for more?

"Now there was a day when his sons and daughters were eating and drinking wine in their oldest brother's house; [14] and a messenger came to Job and said, "The oxen were plowing and the donkeys feeding beside them, [15] when the Sabeans raided them and took them away—indeed they have killed the servants with the edge of the

Deborah G. Hunter

sword; and I alone have escaped to tell you!" ¹⁶ While he was still speaking, another also came and said, "The fire of God fell from heaven and burned up the sheep and the servants, and consumed them; and I alone have escaped to tell you!" ¹⁷ While he was still speaking, another also came and said, "The Chaldeans formed three bands, raided the camels and took them away, yes, and killed the servants with the edge of the sword; and I alone have escaped to tell you!" ¹⁸ While he was still speaking, another also came and said, "Your sons and daughters were eating and drinking wine in their oldest brother's house, ¹⁹ and suddenly a great wind came from across the wilderness and struck the four corners of the house, and it fell on the young people, and they are dead; and I alone have escaped to tell you!" ²⁰ Then Job arose, tore his robe, and shaved his head; and he fell to the ground and worshiped. ²¹ And he said: "Naked I came from my mother's womb, And naked shall I return there. The Lord gave, and the Lord has taken away; Blessed be the name of the Lord." ²² In all this Job did not sin nor charge God with wrong." (Job 1:13-22)

My God! How can someone endure such devastation and still be standing in a place of worship and reverence to the Lord? Job, just as God described him to satan, was a man who respected God and who was blameless in the sight of the Lord. He was tested in his wildernesses and proven ready to receive all that God has released into his hands. He was not a novice to affliction. Job endured many storms before this one hit him. He fell down and worshiped God, because he understood that nothing he had was from his own hand, but solely by the gracious and loving hand of God. The place of maturity Job stood in was matchless! Can you imagine the faces of the men who came to tell him of this tragedy? One by one, they came running to Job in utter

The Wilderness

shock. Before one could finish telling him of a calamity, another would show up with more devastating news.

I realized I was in my first wilderness around 2009. My life went from the greatest high to the greatest low. I sunk daily into loneliness and depression, and I felt as if I would never come out of that pit. Darkness was all around me, and I pondered if I would ever see the Light again. I thought I had lost my salvation, and that God had completely left me alone in this wilderness. I was broken. How could my Father, the One who saved me leave me? Did He not say in His Word that He would never leave me or forsake me? I knew His Word and nothing was lining up for me, because I believed His Word. As I cried out to Him in this dark place, I began to hear that "still small voice". He had not abandoned me. In fact, He led me here to reveal another aspect of Himself to me. After my most intimate times with Him in His presence, and growing tremendously in His Word, He took me to my lowest to let me know that there was more. I didn't think it could get any better than what I had experienced in Germany. My heart and my spirit were opened to the magnificent love of my Father. I witnessed His hand in ways unimaginable, but He knew there was more. God saw what I was prepared for and what I was not. This wilderness revealed a lot to me not only about God, but about me.

The Wilderness of Beersheba is considered the "Place of Surrender". Many times throughout the Word, you will see several people walking through this wilderness, including Hagar, Abraham, Obadiah, and Elijah. One very touching experience was that of Hagar, Abraham's concubine who was summoned by her mistress, Sarah, to conceive a child for them, as Sarah's womb was barren. Hagar willingly agreed, but after a period of time she became indignant with Sarah.

150

Deborah G. Hunter

She began to taunt her mistress by using the child, Ishmael, as a pawn, as she knew Sarah could not conceive a child. Shortly thereafter, the Lord manifested His promise in Sarah's womb, her son Isaac.

As the two brothers began to grow up together, Ishmael began to take on the spirit of his mother Hagar. He started to resent Isaac and his covenant relationship with Abraham. Though he was older, he would not be an heir to his father's kingdom. He despised and made fun of his younger brother, and this infuriated Sarah.

"So the child grew and was weaned. And Abraham made a great feast on the same day that Isaac was weaned. [9] And Sarah saw the son of Hagar the Egyptian, whom she had borne to Abraham, scoffing. [10] Therefore she said to Abraham, "Cast out this bondwoman and her son; for the son of this bondwoman shall not be heir with my son, namely with Isaac." [11] And the matter was very displeasing in Abraham's sight because of his son. [12] But God said to Abraham, "Do not let it be displeasing in your sight because of the lad or because of your bondwoman. Whatever Sarah has said to you, listen to her voice; for in Isaac your seed shall be called. [13] Yet I will also make a nation of the son of the bondwoman, because he is your seed." [14] So Abraham rose early in the morning, and took bread and a skin of water; and putting it on her shoulder, he gave it and the boy to Hagar, and sent her away. Then she departed and wandered in the Wilderness of Beersheba." (Genesis 21:8-14)

Hagar, to some, got the raw end of the deal. She bore a son for Abraham and Sarah, but was ultimately rejected by this family. Unbeknownst to her, and even to Abraham and Sarah, this was all a part of God's plan. Hagar was led into the "Wilderness of Beersheba"

The Wilderness

to surrender to God's plan for her and Ishmael's life. She was holding onto someone else's Promised Land, when God was preparing her own.

"And the water in the skin was used up, and she placed the boy under one of the shrubs. [16] Then she went and sat down across from him at a distance of about a bowshot; for she said to herself, "Let me not see the death of the boy." So she sat opposite him, and lifted her voice and wept. [17] And God heard the voice of the lad. Then the angel of God called to Hagar out of heaven, and said to her, "What ails you, Hagar? Fear not, for God has heard the voice of the lad where he is. [18] Arise, lift up the lad and hold him with your hand, for I will make him a great nation." (Genesis 21:15-18)

Job was beginning to see God in ways he had never before seen Him. Each tragedy he faced produced something greater inside of this servant of God. The multiple trials all at once reveal that Job was a man that satan wanted to destroy. His assignment is to kill, steal, and destroy, but God comes to give us life and life more abundantly. (John 10:10) Satan came back in the midst of the Lord, and God, once again, praised His servant Job for holding fast to his integrity. Satan, bent at destroying this man, told God that if He stretched out His hand against him and touched his bone and his flesh, that Job would curse God to His face. God permitted the enemy to test Job once again. Quick note here, God does not put sickness and disease on anyone. Satan was not only trying to destroy Job, but he

> The enemy will always try to find ways to taint the name and character of God.

152

Deborah G. Hunter

had the nerve to ask the Lord to do something that is out of His character to do. The enemy will always try to find ways to taint the name and character of God. But he is no match for our Lord and Savior, Jesus Christ!

The enemy went out and did was he was "allowed" to do, all in an effort to prove that Job was who God said he was. Satan went and struck Job with boils from the top of his head to the bottom of his feet. He was in tremendous pain, and even went as far as to get a potsherd to scrape himself with. A potsherd was a broken piece of ceramic material, normally used during that time in water pots or cooking vessels. How in the world could someone stand the pain of boils from head to toe, let alone scraping them off with sharp, ceramic pieces? His wife had come to her own breaking point. She wife asked him, "Do you still hold fast to your integrity? Curse God and die." (Job 2:9) Job's response was epic!

"But he said to her, "You speak as one of the foolish women speaks. Shall we indeed accept good from God, and shall we not accept adversity?" In all this Job did not sin with his lips." (Job 2:10)

What faithfulness displayed during one of the most painful times in his life! I have to say that I am not without empathy for Job. My entire Christian walk has been riddled with sickness and disease. In fact, at this very moment, in the writing of this book, I have experienced some of the greatest attacks on my health, as well as my mind. God spoke to me on New Year's Eve of 2013 that I needed to start writing again. It had been seven years since I had written last, at the inception of this book. This was truly my time in the wilderness. I began to write this book in January of 2014. It was truly a struggle to

The Wilderness

even begin. Distraction upon distraction surfaced, and I almost gave up many times. I set a three month deadline, which was never a problem before, as each of my books was written in just several short months. This was different in every aspect! I began to get very tired each time I picked this book up to write. This was not a normal feeling of begin sleepy, this was exhaustion, as if I had run a marathon. As time progressed, I began to get sharp pains in my chest during this time of putting pen to paper. I had to get up and walk around my house, as it was surely not normal. After about two weeks of this happening, only when I wrote, I really began to get worried. I prayed, anointed myself with oil and laid hands upon myself, declaring healing over my body. These pains eventually ceased.

I was into the second month of writing when I began to develop severe anxiety attacks while driving to our church in Denver. Mind you, I have never had anxiety attacks in my life. Also, we had been driving back and forth three to five days a week for two years. I love driving! I absolutely dream of road trips, and the peacefulness that comes over me while driving. This is usually some of my greatest times of intimacy with the Lord. So, I immediately sensed that this was an attack. If I got up past a certain speed, my heart would begin to race and my hands sweat. I was forced to slow down to the point where cars were flying past me beeping their horns. If I went around a slight curve, I felt as if I was going to flip my truck. My daughter witnessed this more times than I can count during this time. Week after week, it became worse and I literally thought I would die on these roads. Mind you, a year earlier, a beautiful sister sent me an email. We do not know one another personally, but through social media, we have come to be great sisters in the Lord. She sent me a message stating that the Lord spoke a very specific word to her about me. She proceeded to tell me that God said He would watch over my family and me on the road-ways, as we traveled to church, that I did not have to worry about ice, rain, snow, or any other weather system. His angels would watch over us. Not a "super spiritual" word, just a word of peace and comfort.

Little did she know, as I received this message, we were travel-ing back from our church in Denver during one of the worst snow-storms that year. Cars were sliding off the road in front of us and behind us. We could go no more than thirty-forty miles an hour to avoid sliding, and this even seemed too fast. The snow was coming down so fast that you could not even see the marker lines on the road. I happened to check my phone while we were at a standstill, and there was one message blinking. I viewed it, and it was from this precious woman of God. Peace flooded my heart, and at that moment, I knew God was with us and would continue to watch over us, just as He promised. So, in this season of anxiety attacks, I began to give Him back His Word. I started to declare His promises over my life, and I had several people covering me in prayer during this time.

I wish I could say this was all I experienced, but it was just the beginning. Shortly after this, we moved into our new home. A time that should have been the most exciting time, as God was opening up doors unimaginable for my family, became a time of great darkness for me. Several prophetic words came forth in our lives, and they surfaced very quickly. Four of eight doors prophesied opened within one week! We were elated and praising God for His Word. Shortly after this, I got sick. I was having hard time breathing as I lay in bed at night, and this was not a "cold" issue. I was gasping for breath and had to jump up each night it occurred. I would prop my head up, so the elevation would help me breathe better. Nothing was helping. The anxiety

The Wilderness

attacks that surfaced on the roadways now entered my home. I honestly thought I was dying. Some nights, I would lay awake all night, fighting the urge to fall asleep. Fear entered my heart, and I was sure if I closed my eyes, I would not wake up. I began to think about how my family would wake up and find me dead. As I closed my eyes, I would have visions of darkness and floating through the clouds. I was truly being tormented by demonic spirits. As a Christian, many would assume we cannot be affected by such, but just as we see with Job, I believe God allows the enemy to do such, in order to bring us out of our wildernesses greater than when we entered. Again, I know the testimony and impact of this book will be to the glory of God!

I shared this with a dear mentor of mine that has covered me and spoken into and over my life for several years now. He is a phenomenal leader, both spiritually and business-wise, a missionary to more nations that I can count, dean of a theology school, and liaison to many kings, prime ministers, presidents and leaders all over the world. We met in Germany, and he was instrumental in prophesying much of what God is now doing in and through me at this very moment. I trust what he speaks into life. His ministry is tested and proven. These were his exact words to me, "Deborah, this sounds much bigger than a mere seasonal attack. It's a ploy to destroy you, and I agree with you that it just might be spiritual."

What Job was going through was spiritual, though it touched his physical body, and it had purpose. God Himself had orchestrated this testing. He allowed the enemy to touch everything that concerned Job. If you are going through something similar, know that it is for a reason far greater than what you can imagine. You have not sinned,

Deborah G. Hunter

you have not fallen away from God, and you are NOT crazy! You have been found faithful, and God is preparing you for your next level.

"Have I sinned? What have I done to You, O watcher of men? Why have You set me as Your target, So that I am a burden to myself?" (Job 7:20)

You must prepare yourself for great persecution and testing during your wilderness times. Many people will not understand what you are going through. In fact, some will form their own opinions of why you are going through so much turmoil, including thinking you are in some sort of sin, disobedience, rebellion, or that you have turned away from the Lord.

Be very mindful of people who will judge you during your times of testing in the wilderness. Though they, too, are assigned to be a part of your testing, but you must understand that they will go no further than your wilderness. Don't bring "wilderness" people into your Promised Land. They were only meant to be seasonal tools in the hand of God to propel you towards your destiny!

> Don't bring "wilderness" people into your Promised Land.

Job understood this better than most. Not only did his wife give up on him, but so did his friends. There are very few that God has placed in your life to cover you during these times of testing, and many times, you may never even know who they are. Your wilderness is a time of isolation, loneliness, and preparation. God has to remove people from

The Wilderness

your life, so that He alone receives your full and undivided attention. He does not want you to depend upon anyone but Him.

Each of Job's friends, Eliphaz, Bildad, and Zophar, assumed they knew what God was doing in Job's life. They all gave their interpretations of his suffering, one to the point of offering a prophetic 'dream' to shed light on his afflictions. People will assume they know what God is doing in your life, when in reality, that have no earthly clue what He is doing, and that their assumptions and accusations are ultimately a part of His plan as well. God will eventually cause your enemies and accusers to watch you become elevated, and they will have to sit and watch while you eat at the table the Lord prepares for you. (Psalm 23:5) Those who oppress you will have to prepare a sacrifice for you, just as Job's friends were required of the Lord to do so.

Eliphaz:
"Remember now, who ever perished being innocent?
Or where were the upright ever cut off?
⁸ Even as I have seen,
Those who plow iniquity
And sow trouble reap the same." (Job 4:7-8)

Bildad:
"If you would earnestly seek God
And make your supplication to the Almighty,
⁶ If you were pure and upright,
Surely now He would awake for you,
And prosper your rightful dwelling place." (Job 8:5-6)

Deborah G. Hunter

Zophar:

For you have said, 'My doctrine is pure, And I am clean in your eyes.' [5] But oh, that God would speak, And open His lips against you, [6 That] He would show you the secrets of wisdom! For they would double your prudence. Know therefore that God exacts from you less than your iniquity deserves. (Job 11:4-6)

Every one of them accused Job of some sort of iniquity. Iniquity means great injustice or an extremely immoral act, grossly immoral. Why would God say what He said in Job Chapter one if Job was found an immoral man, a man in deep immorality? Remember what God said, "Have you considered my *servant* Job, a man *blameless* and *upright*, and one who *feared God* and *shunned evil*." This was surely not punishment for iniquity or immorality; this was a proving of who God said he was to the enemy, as well as revealing the glory of God through Job's tests. Don't worry about who others say you are, or what they think you are going through. In the end, God will receive the glory for your life, and everyone who spoke out against you will have to watch the Lord elevate you for His magnificent purposes!

Job's response was fairly long. He pretty much laid his friends out. He was baffled at how they could accuse him, instead of comfort him. But the one statement that rises above all the rest is, "Though He slay me, yet will I trust Him." (Job 14:15) Job was confident in his relationship with God, and he knew he was blameless and an upright man, one who feared God and shunned evil. So he would plead his case, even if it meant death. He trusted that whatever was happening, God was still in control His friends continued to mock him and accuse him. All of which was in God's plan for Job's process of preparation, his wilderness.

The Wilderness

"O earth, do not cover my blood, And let my cry have no resting place! [19] Surely even now my witness is in heaven, And my evidence is on high. [20] My friends scorn me; My eyes pour out tears to God. [21] Oh, that one might plead for a man with God, As a man pleads for his neighbor!" (Job 16:18-21)

Job was crying out for someone to plead to the Lord on his behalf. I remember, all too well, this feeling in my wilderness. People who spoke so highly of me in the past were now accusing me of some of the very same things Job was accused of by his friends. Almost instantly, people were coming up against me who were just building me up days earlier? I felt so betrayed and confused. I did not understand then that this was God's doing.

"He has removed my brothers far from me, And my acquaintances are completely estranged from me. [14] My relatives have failed, And my close friends have forgotten me." (Job 19:13-14)

It had nothing to do with my innocence, but all to do with His purpose for my wilderness. Job trusted God, even when He did not understand. I, too, found this place of solace, eventually. I was still hurt and even to this day, saddened by the loss of relationships, but I trust my Father. I trust that He knows the length of my days, the steps of my path, and the people who will walk along this journey with me...He is ordering my very footsteps and yours too.

"But He knows the way that I take; When He has tested me, I shall come forth as gold." (Job 23:10)

160

Deborah G. Hunter

Brokenness leads to a place of beauty in our lives. Through all of the devastation in Job's wilderness, his children dying, his possessions stripped from his hands, the afflictions put upon him by the enemy, and the accusations hurled at him from his friends, Job still found himself grounded in his faith in God and the love His Lord had for him.

"God uses broken things. It takes broken soil to produce a crop, broken clouds to give rain, broken grain to give bread, broken bread to give strength. It is the broken alabaster box that gives forth perfume. It is Peter, weeping bitterly, who returns to greater power than ever."
— Vance Havner

What a beautiful analogy of brokenness. Without it in our lives, we will never truly see the beauty of the fruit produced from it. It is in the crushing of olives where the purest form of olive oil is fashioned. The anointing is formed in our lives through the tests, trials, and tribulation that we endure. Our Lord and Savior was crushed, bruised, beaten, whipped, scourged, and ripped apart. His body was broken for us. In His brokenness, the glory of God was revealed to the world. Some only see the gruesome picture of a lifeless body hanging on the cross, but I see the "beauty of brokenness" in a Son who submitted and gave His life, so that many other sons could live in eternity with their Father.

> Brokenness leads to a place of beauty in our lives.

Job was restored by God and blessed more in his latter days than in his former. His time in his wilderness revealed a more intimate

The Wilderness

trust and relationship with God, and produced even more beauty in the life of this servant. His friends, family, and neighbors witnessed valuable life lessons through his tests, and their lives, just as Job's, were never the same.

Who will enter into eternity through your willingness to allow brokenness to have its work in your life? Through your exit out of your wilderness, how many others will see the glory of God revealed through your life? This is much bigger than just a test for us; it is plan for many more to come to the saving knowledge of Jesus Christ through our submitted lives. We are called to lay down our lives and take up our cross just as Jesus did. The ground has to be broken in order for seed to be planted, and it has to break again for that harvest to spring forth. Don't despise the process. Allow the pain of your preparation to be the catalyst to propel you towards your Promised Land! There is Beauty in Brokenness! You are a son of God!

Chapter Tips

#30: God Can Make A Way Where There Seems None

When you reach the point where absolutely no one and nothing can help your situation, what then? Where do you go and who are you going to call? It is said that human extremity is frequently the meeting place with God. It makes for an unmatched rendezvous point with divinity. The Psalmist wrote: "I look up to the mountains—does my help come from there? My help comes from the Lord, who made the heavens and the earth" (Psalm 121:1-2 NLT) ~Dr. Dennis Sempebwa

#31: There are some tests we will not understand. Trust Him and watch Him reveal His glory!

God never reveals everything to us. He understands if we have knowledge of each step, we would run as fast as we could in the other direction. You don't have to have all of the answers, just put your full trust in Him, and follow blindly. There is such a precious faith that is developed during these times of brokenness. The Word says that the secret things belong to God, but there are certain things that will be revealed. Some things are on a "need to know basis".

The Wilderness

#32: Brokenness is essential to entering our Promised Land.

If we are to walk in the fullness of God and enter into His divine purposes for our lives, we have to die to our flesh. Self cannot enter the Kingdom. Your wilderness is designed to purge you of everything that is not of God. Let go and let God!

#33: He is the potter, and we are the clay!

Allow the Lord to mold you into a vessel He can use for His glory. It is no longer about what you want, but wholly what He desires for your life. He is able to do exceeding, abundantly; above all we could ask or think. Your end looks magnificent!

"that their hearts may be
encouraged, being knit together in
love, and attaining to all riches of
the full assurance of understanding,
to the knowledge of the mystery of
God, both of the Father and of
Christ,"

Ephesians3:20

Chapter 10

Lord, What is Happening to Me? Calvary's Hill

"The Wilderness of Damascus"
(The Place of Encouragement)

"and sent Timothy, our brother and minister of God, and our fellow laborer in the gospel of Christ, to establish you and encourage you concerning your faith," (1 Thessalonians 3:2)

The final wilderness we will study is the Wilderness of Damascus. This wilderness represents the "Place of Encouragement". In our wilderness journey's, the one thing most needed is that of encouragement. For us to press forward and walk through these necessary tests, we need to be encouraged, whether that is through the Word, prayer,

The Wilderness

or from those who have faithfully endured their own wilderness experiences. Encouragement is crucial if we are going to walk successfully through our wilderness and into our Promised Land. Elijah was considered one of the greatest prophets of all time. In fact, he is one of the three standing on the Mount of Configuration, along with Moses and Jesus, as our Lord was seen in His glory by the three disciples Peter, John, and James. Elijah was one of few people who were "translated," or taken up, by God into Heaven; he did not see a physical death.

> Encouragement is crucial if we are going to walk successfully through our wilderness and into our Promised Land.

Elijah's name means "Jehovah is God". He was a man of great faith, boldness, and courage. This prophet of God heard the voice of the Lord and was obedient to carry out every word. In his obedience to God in delivering a word to Ahab, God led Elijah to refreshing. He was directed towards the brook of Cherith where he received water. God provided bread and meat through the mouths of ravens every day until the brook of water dried up. Elijah knew God as Jehovah, in this case, Jehovah Jireh, the Lord His provider. His walk with the Lord revealed that God was with him every step of the way, to the widow of Zarephath who provided for him, to the miracle of unending oil and meal for him, the widow, and her son, as well as the Lord using Elijah to raise this boy from the dead. Miracle after miracle was seen through the life of this amazing prophet of God. Most remarkably is the miracle of rain that came in a season of great famine.

Deborah G. Hunter

The prophet once again opened his mouth in obedience to the Lord concerning Ahab and his people. He was confident, bold, and unashamed to speak what the Lord was saying, a true prophet among prophets.

"Then it happened, when Ahab saw Elijah, that Ahab said to him, "Is that you, O troubler of Israel?" [18] And he answered, "I have not troubled Israel, but you and your father's house have, in that you have forsaken the commandments of the Lord and have followed the Baals. [19] Now therefore, send and gather all Israel to me on Mount Carmel, the four hundred and fifty prophets of Baal, and the four hundred prophets of Asherah, who eat at Jezebel's table." (1 Kings 18:17-19)

What boldness in the face of adversity! Elijah confidently articulated to Ahab what the Lord was saying. Ahab heeded Elijah's words and summoned the eight-hundred and fifty prophets to Mount Carmel. Now I don't know how many men would even get to this point? Nowhere does it say that Elijah had any troops, companions, or other prophets with him; he was alone! And here he is summoning over eight-hundred and fifty men to meet him. Elijah could have been killed on the spot with Ahab, and most assuredly on this mountain with a troop of men, but the hand of God was upon this prophet.

"So Ahab sent for all the children of Israel, and gathered the prophets together on Mount Carmel.[21] And Elijah came to all the people, and said, "How long will you falter between two opinions? If the Lord is God, follow Him; but if Baal, follow him." But the people answered him not a word. [22] Then Elijah said to the people, "I alone am left a prophet of the Lord; but Baal's prophets are four hundred and

The Wilderness

fifty men. [23] Therefore let them give us two bulls; and let them choose one bull for themselves, cut it in pieces, and lay it on the wood, but put no fire under it; and I will prepare the other bull, and lay it on the wood, but put no fire under it. [24] Then you call on the name of your gods, and I will call on the name of the Lord; and the God who answers by fire, He is God."

So all the people answered and said, "It is well spoken."

[25] Now Elijah said to the prophets of Baal, "Choose one bull for yourselves and prepare it first, for you are many; and call on the name of your god, but put no fire under it."

[26] So they took the bull which was given them, and they prepared it, and called on the name of Baal from morning even till noon, saying, "O Baal, hear us!" But there was no voice; no one answered. Then they leaped about the altar which they had made.

[27] And so it was, at noon, that Elijah mocked them and said, "Cry aloud, for he is a god; either he is meditating, or he is busy, or he is on a journey, or perhaps he is sleeping and must be awakened." [28] So they cried aloud, and cut themselves, as was their custom, with knives and lances, until the blood gushed out on them. [29] And when midday was past, they prophesied until the time of the offering of the evening sacrifice. But there was no voice; no one answered, no one paid attention.

[30] Then Elijah said to all the people, "Come near to me." So all the people came near to him. And he repaired the altar of the Lord that was broken down. [31] And Elijah took twelve stones, according to the number of the tribes of the sons of Jacob, to whom the word of the Lord had come, saying, "Israel shall be your name." [32] Then with the stones he built an altar in the name of the Lord; and he made a trench around the altar large enough to hold two seahs of seed. [33] And he put the wood in order, cut the bull in pieces, and laid it on the

wood, and said, "Fill four waterpots with water, and pour it on the burnt sacrifice and on the wood." [34] Then he said, "Do it a second time," and they did it a second time; and he said, "Do it a third time," and they did it a third time. [35] So the water ran all around the altar; and he also filled the trench with water.

[36] And it came to pass, at the time of the offering of the evening sacrifice, that Elijah the prophet came near and said, "Lord God of Abraham, Isaac, and Israel, let it be known this day that You are God in Israel and I am Your servant, and that I have done all these things at Your word. [37] Hear me, O Lord, hear me, that this people may know that You are the Lord God, and that You have turned their hearts back to You again."

[38] Then the fire of the Lord fell and consumed the burnt sacrifice, and the wood and the stones and the dust, and it licked up the water that was in the trench. [39] Now when all the people saw it, they fell on their faces; and they said, "The Lord, He is God! The Lord, He is God!"

[40] And Elijah said to them, "Seize the prophets of Baal! Do not let one of them escape!" So they seized them; and Elijah brought them down to the Brook Kishon and executed them there." (1 Kings 18:20-40)

Elijah's experience in this wilderness is probably one of the most notable in scripture. He fled to the "Wilderness of Damascus" after he had one of the greatest victories of his life. He had killed over four-hundred and fifty prophets of Baal. Ahab shared Elijah's feat with his wife, Jezebel, and she vowed to kill Elijah by that same time the next day.

The Wilderness

"And when he saw that, he arose, and went for his life, and came to Beersheba, which belongeth to Judah, and left his servant there. But he himself went a day's journey into the wilderness, and came and sat down under a juniper tree: and he requested for himself that he might die; and said, It is enough; now, O LORD, take away my life; for I am not better than my fathers." (1 Kings 19:3-4)

Elijah was tired. How could someone who had just defeated four-hundred and fifty prophets be afraid of one woman? This spirit of intimidation, from Jezebel, caught him at one of his most vulnerable moments. He was spiritually, emotionally, and physically depleted, so he ran. He asked the Lord to take his life, but God knew Elijah was just exhausted. In the proceeding verses, the Lord refreshed the man of God and prepared him for his next assignment.

> He was spiritually, emotionally, and physically depleted, so he ran.

"Then as he lay and slept under a broom tree, suddenly an angel touched him, and said to him, "Arise and eat." [6] Then he looked, and there by his head was a cake baked on coals, and a jar of water. So he ate and drank, and lay down again. [7] And the angel of the Lord came back the second time, and touched him, and said, "Arise and eat, because the journey is too great for you." [8] So he arose, and ate and drank; and he went in the strength of that food forty days and forty nights as far as Horeb, the mountain of God." (1 Kings 19:5-8)

Many times, we are led into our wilderness because we need to be refreshed. We have fought many spiritual battles, and need to be

Deborah G. Hunter

replenished. We need to saturate ourselves in the Word of God (eat), allow the Spirit of God to refill our lives (drink), and to lay down in His presence and be still (rest). We are continuously being prepared for each journey, or assignment, in Christ. Be sure to stay refreshed and continue to allow the Lord to pour back into you, or you will not have anything to pour out, and you will become worn out from serving and helping God's people.

"The Lord said to him, "Go, return on your way to the wilderness of Damascus, and when you have arrived, you shall anoint Hazael king over Aram;" (1 Kings 19:15)

After the Lord had strengthened Elijah by providing food, drink, and rest, he fled into a cave after journeying for forty days and forty nights. This is a prophetic mirror of the wandering of the children of Israel on their way to the Promised Land. We also see the testing of our Lord and Savior, Jesus Christ, in Matthew as fulfilled prophecy of this shadow text in Elijah. He, too, was tested by the enemy, but the Word said he "fasted," or chose, to discipline himself for forty days and forty nights in the wilderness, and afterwards, it said he was hungry and that angels ministered to Him. What was Elijah doing, or not doing, that caused so much anxiety and fear in his life? Had Elijah strayed away from the spiritual disciplines of reading, fasting, and praying? Were the miracles and spiritual victories becoming such a norm for him that he just expected God to sustain him? Was he so used to hearing God for the supernatural miracles and victories that he was unable to hear Him when He was calling him to rest?

"Then He said, "Go out, and stand on the mountain before the Lord." And behold, the Lord passed by, and a great and strong

173

The Wilderness

wind tore into the mountains and broke the rocks in pieces before the Lord, but the Lord was not in the wind; and after the wind an earthquake, but the Lord was not in the earthquake; [12] and after the earthquake a fire, but the Lord was not in the fire; and after the fire a still small voice." (1 Kings 19:11)

Elijah was used to hearing God in the "big things," but God was trying to train his ear to hear Him when there was no "special assignment" to fulfill. Elijah had become so used to being "used" by the Lord that he began to feel his victories were coming by his own strength. It had come to a point where anxiety and fear took such a hold of his heart and his mind that he felt he was the only one left who was for the Lord. God encouraged Elijah that he was not alone in this journey, that there were seven thousand believers who had not bowed to Baal.

I can't judge Elijah by thinking he was the only one left to carry on the torch for the Lord. I, too, have felt this way many times. In serving the Lord wholeheartedly and engaging in spiritual warfare through prayer and intercession for so long, I had

> So many spiritual leaders and ministers of the Gospel are getting burned out, because they are not receiving the rest of the Lord.

become weary. Not understanding that I needed the rest of the Lord, I continued steadfast in the work of God. If Jesus needed to get away from the crowds, the miracles, and the "hoopla" and go to the mountaintop to fast and pray, so too do we. So many spiritual leaders and ministers of the Gospel are getting burned out, because they are not receiving the rest of the Lord. They are operating on fumes and the words of yesteryear to sustain them. We need to take time away from the ministry, with family, friends, and yes, in quiet times of rest, relaxation, and renewal in the Word of God, fasting, and prayer. And others need to respect this, and allow room for it, so that we can be refreshed. If you continue to pull on your man or woman of God and expect them to be everywhere all of the time, they will become exhausted and frustrated, because they are operating off of flesh and not the Spirit of God. "'Not by might, nor by power, but by My Spirit,' says the Lord of hosts." (Zechariah 4:6)

We cannot do the will or work of the Lord in and of our own strength or power. We have to depend fully and totally upon His Spirit abiding within us to accomplish the assignments we are called to fulfill. Jesus, on His way to Calvary, stopped in the Garden of Gethsemane to pray. The Bible says that He sweat droplets of blood because he was so troubled and distressed with sorrow. He prayed that God would take this suffering from Him, but even if He did not, His will was more important than the temporary affliction He had to endure. The suffering and sacrifice of Jesus allowed the Holy Spirit to be poured out on those who believe in Him.

The word Gethsemane is a Hebrew word derived from two roots, Gat and Shmanim, meaning "the place where olive oil is pressed". At an olive press, olives are gathered into rough sacks and stacked on top of one another. Pressure was added to the end of the beam to press oil from the olives. The more pressure; the more oil. Olive oil symbolizes the presence of the Spirit of God. It was also used to bring light from the menorah in the Tabernacle into the wilderness.

The Wilderness

Elijah's Calvary was in the Wilderness of Damascus. He was being pressed in the fire of affliction in his mind, but through each season of rest, he was being reinforced by the Spirit of God for his assignments. The light of God was being restored to his soul. Jesus' press in the garden produced the presence of God needed to continue on His journey to Golgotha. Joseph, though in a pit with no water, generated a praise in his heart that summoned the God of Heaven to hear his cry and send a band of Ishmaelites to pull him out of his darkness. David, in the deep jaws of Saul's vengeance, loosed his servant's heart and activated the presence of God into his life. The woman at the well, though silent, was prodded and persecuted by hypocrites, but drew from the well of Living Water and was never the same again. Deborah and Ja'el, in the midst of a male-dominated society, possessed such grace and wisdom through submission and honor to their husbands that God placed victory in their hands. The children of Israel wandered aimlessly for forty years, and many died in their wilderness, but some endured till the end and witnessed their Promised Land. Samson, though blinded by the Philistines, saw better in darkness than he did in light. In the darkest season of his life, he was finally able to see God's purpose. Solomon's lust for wealth, status, fame, and women cost him his kingdom, but God did not cut him off completely. He left a portion of the kingdom to his son, because of His covenant with David. God's mercy is endless! Job was stripped of everything precious to him: his children, his home, his property, his livestock, his business, his wealth, and his health. In his brokenness, God restored it all back to him! He received double for his trouble! And finally, Elijah, the poignant Prophet. His exploits preceded him, but it was in the quiet chambers of his mind, while resting and refueling, that he received the strength and encouragement to continue in his assignment.

Deborah G. Hunter

DON'T QUIT!!! Elijah went from a spirit of euphoria into a deep pit of depression, feeling like he was the only one left to defend God before the heathen. What happens when great victories don't end up how we expect them to? It can become place where we lose faith and hit rock bottom. It is a position where your faith is not placed upon God, but on "your" knowledge of God and what He has done previously in your life. This mighty man of immense faith, a great heroic prophet, was now afraid and running. He had lost faith in God and looked to his strength, which was limited, to defeat Jezebel and her army of false prophets. God sent him back to remind Elijah of His goodness and faithfulness; He reminded him to put full trust in Him. God starts with the physical and emotional needs before he deals

> We are sent into our wildernesses because this is the place where we are able to hear the 'still small voice'.

with the spiritual. We are sent into our wildernesses because this is the place where we are able to hear the 'still small voice'. This is the place where God moves the greatest, when our awakened conscious becomes the most powerful force in the world. God usually works when things are at an apparent standstill. When God seems to be doing nothing, the greatest things are taking place. A changed attitude is often the key to a transformed life.

Elijah finally stopped running long enough to hear the voice of God. It was in this place that he received the instructions to move forward in his assignments. Will you stop running? Are you willing to lay aside the "work of the ministry" to truly hear what God is saying to you now? Not what He spoke to you twenty years ago, ten years ago,

The Wilderness

five years ago, or even last year, but what is God saying now? We all need to remain pliable to the Spirit of God. Take the chains off of Holy Spirit. Loose the shackles of self-reliance, and allow the Lord to have His way in your life. You are not called to be in control. You are not commanded to make the decisions that only God can make. You are commissioned to follow His leading, through His example, so that lives can be touched, healed, delivered, set free, and saved. Our ultimate example is Jesus Christ, and He endured every wilderness that we will ever face. He went *through* His wilderness to encourage us that we, too, can make it *through* ours. He earned the reward of being a Son. "This is my beloved Son in whom I am well pleased." Embrace the process of your preparation, so you can walk into your Promised Land. The manifestation of the sons!

Chapter Tips

#35: Rest in absolutely pertinent to the life of a Believer.

You are not a super-hero and you are not God! The same way you need to refuel in the spiritual disciplines of reading, fasting, and praying, you need to replenish your physical body in the natural through rest.

#36: Encouragement is essential to maintaining a healthy balance in your assignment.

You are not alone in the Kingdom. God would never put so much pressure upon one person, except His Son Jesus Christ who carried the weight of the world upon His shoulders. Do your part, stay close to the Lord, and finish YOUR race. There is a crown awaiting your faithfulness!

#37: Be sure that your victories don't silence the voice that is crying out from the wilderness.

Winning battles for Christ is a phenomenal feeling, but never allow the "bells of battle" to out-ring the voice of God in your life. Keep in mind that there are many more battles to fight, so keep the lines of communication open between you and God.

The Wilderness

#38: Though God is BIG, He is normally NOT in big things.

God is a jealous God. He loves to bless His people, and His desire is for us to know Him, but He doesn't use all of the "bells and whistles" we do in ministry to prove that He is God. Elijah was used in great miracles, but the signs & wonders were not for his benefit, but for the unbelieving false prophets. We know God through His Word and His love for us. He speaks in the "small" things, and we are required to learn how to discern His voice. He was not in the wind, not in the earthquake, and not in the fire...He came with a "still small voice". Listen.

#39: Remember what God has done for you.

God provided so many times for Elijah before this great feat with the prophets of Baal. He fed him by the brook of Cherith through ravens, He supplied food for Elijah, the widow, and her son, He provided oil overflowing that allowed the woman and her son to live, and He brought forth rain after a six year drought. Never forget what God has done for you throughout your life. And also never forget that it was Him doing it. When we stop thanking Him and reverencing Him, we take credit for the wonders He performs in our lives.

#40: Embrace your wilderness!

Your wilderness is not meant to destroy you; it is designed to propel you toward your Promise!

"I knew you in the wilderness, In the land of great drought.

Hosea 13:5

Epilogue

If we read and meditate upon the Bible intentionally, we cannot help but see the many instances in scripture that point to the wilderness. The Old Testament is laced with the children of Israel wandering from wilderness to wilderness, in search of some sort of fulfillment. Elijah fell into the intimidating trap of Jezebel while exhausted and fled into the wilderness in great distress and depression. David spent many days and nights in the wilderness, running from the hand of King Saul. Even Jesus spent forty days in the wilderness before He was released to perform the supernatural miracles of the Bible. In these many examples, we must assume that at some point along our journey, each of us will experience our own wilderness.

To walk fully in our purpose, we must seek to gain a better understanding of the true importance of the "wilderness". The wilderness is a place where our natural senses are commanded to submit to the spiritual. It is in our willingness to crucify our flesh during these seasons that our spiritual senses are heightened, and we become indebted to the Spirit of God within. We hear so often, "Let go and let God!" This could not be a more authentic statement concerning the wilderness. He is the One who leads us all into our seasons of testing.

The Wilderness

God is the orchestrator of our footsteps, and if we allow Him to lead us, we can see the beauty of every test and trial we go through in our wilderness.

Every believer passes through what may be described as wilderness experiences. Each of us must be put to the test of our faith. We have to know who God is in our lives, and many times, we have to be reminded through the ways of the wilderness. The wilderness serves not only as a place of desolation and famine, but also a place of nourishment, testing, and revelation, and a framework for true transformation. I cringe when I hear people say we no longer need to go through the wilderness, because we are a part of the New Covenant church, and we entered our Promised Land through the death and resurrection of Jesus Christ. Why would He reveal so many instances in the Word God about the necessity of the wilderness if He did not require each of us to experience it? It is pride and arrogance to think we have "arrived" and that we don't need to go through conversion. Is that not the goal? To be transformed by the renewing of our mind?

The place that seems to be the most difficult, the darkest, and the most confusing we have ever experienced in our lives, can also become the place where we encounter the true and living God of our salvation. We must look at our situations with different eyes. Not everything that looks good is God, but more importantly, not everything that feels bad is of the devil. God allows tests to produce a greater harvest of fruit in our lives. These experiences are times of great growth, and the very place that seems void of all hope and light is really a doorway to your destiny! We can liken this to the journey a baby takes through the vestibule of the womb. It is a dark, narrow pathway through the birth canal. It is being forced into a position that

Deborah G. Hunter

begins to squeeze, and makes the baby uncomfortable. It is leaving its natural surroundings and what is "comfortable" to him, and is uncertain of what is to come on the other side. But once its head crowns and breaks forth through the atrium of life, the *light* fills everything inside of that child. It cries, it trembles, and is afraid. The light agitates the baby's eyes and it may take a few minutes, but now they can finally see. Once they adapt to their new surroundings, we see the smile of hope, and love immeasurable.

Faith cannot be explained. We are entering a place never before encountered. A place of peace, rest, and abundant life! But we have to understand that there is a process. We must go through the wilderness first, in order to walk into the blessing and prosperity of God, or we will find ourselves replacing the Giver with the gifts. Hold fast to your process and stay close in the presence of the Lord. Greater things are in store for those who faithfully endure and persevere in the midst of adversity. God is preparing you to be a son. He is producing beauty inside of you beyond what you could ever imagine. Your process in the wilderness is producing a far more lasting reward than just temporary happiness and earthly reward. God wants to use you to bring more people into His Kingdom. He wants your life to impact this world for Jesus Christ! The world is awaiting the manifestation of the sons of God! You are a son!

"A highway shall be there, and a road, And it shall be called the Highway of Holiness. The unclean shall not pass over it, But it shall be for others. Whoever walks the road, although a fool, Shall not go astray." Isaiah 35:8

"Who is this coming up from the wilderness,
Leaning upon her Beloved?"

(Song of Solomon 8:5)

About the Author

Deborah G. Hunter is a wife, mother, author, inspirational speaker, and CEO & Publisher of Hunter Heart Publishing. She has written three books of her own, *Breaking the Eve Mentality*, *Raising Your Prophet*, and *The Call of Intercession*. Deborah travels nationally & internationally on her mission to "Offer God's Heart to a Dying World" through the inspired gift of writing, personal testimony, and through the gifts God has placed in her. She serves as an avid philanthropist through her charity, Stir Up the Gift, dedicated to providing support for the needy around the world, including the country of Japan after the wake of the 2011 Earthquake/Tsunami that ravaged this country.

Deborah has been a born-again believer since the age of twelve and has been on her pathway to destiny ever since. She was ordained as a Minister on July 7, 2007 in Kitzingen, Germany under Drs Will & Kristie Moreland of International Gospel Church. She received her Bachelor's of Arts Degree in Biblical Studies/Theology from Minnesota Graduate School of Theology, and is now an Elder at The Potter's House of Denver under the covering of Dr. Chris & Lady Joy Hill.

Deborah is married to Chris Hunter, Jr., radio personality and CEO of Hunter Entertainment Network, a conglomerate of Christian media outlets, including record label, movie, book, and music production companies. They share in the raising of their three children together, Jade, Elijah, and Ja'el, and are the father and step-mother of three, along with three beautiful grandchildren.

OTHER BOOKS BY
DEBORAH G. HUNTER
AVAILABLE NOW AT
WWW.HUNTERHEARTPUBLISHING.COM
AMAZON.COM, BARNES & NOBLE
AND ALL MAJOR CHRISTIAN BOOKSTORES
AND OUTLETS WORLDWIDE!

website: www.hunterheartpublishing.com
Facebook: Deborah G. Hunter
Twitter: @hunterheartpub
YouTube: Hunter Heart Publishing

OTHER BOOKS BY
DEBORAH G. HUNTER
COMING SOON!

THE
WILDERNESS
SERIES

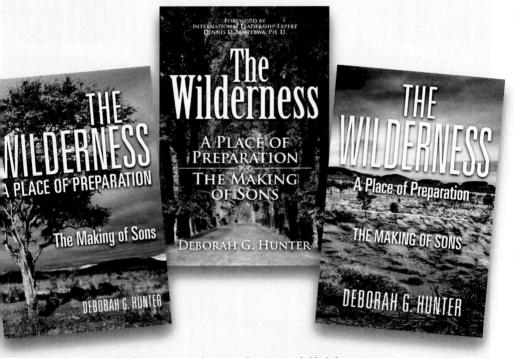

website: www.hunterheartpublishing.com
Facebook: Deborah G. Hunter
Twitter: @hunterheartpub
YouTube: Hunter Heart Publishing

OTHER BOOKS BY
DEBORAH G. HUNTER
COMING SOON!

website: www.hunterheartpublishing.com
Facebook: Deborah G. Hunter
Twitter: @hunterheartpub
YouTube: Hunter Heart Publishing

PRAYER FOR SALVATION

"God, I come to You in the Name of Jesus. I ask You to come into my life. I confess with my mouth that Jesus is my Lord and I believe in my heart that You have raised Him from the dead. I turn my back on sin and I commit to follow You for the rest of my life. I thank You, Father, for saving me!"

If you have prayed this prayer for the first time, we would love to hear from you. You can email us at publisher@hunterheartpublishing.com and we would love to pray with you and help you to find a local church to get connected to.

Contact us:

Hunter Heart Publishing™
4164 Austin Bluffs Parkway, Suite 214
Colorado Springs, Colorado 80918

publisher@hunterheartpublishing.com

(253) 906-2160

www.hunterheartpublishing.com